SACRAMENTS in the NEW LITURGY

Rev. B.D. Killeen

OUR SUNDAY VISITOR, INC.
NOLL PLAZA, HUNTINGTON, INDIANA 46750

Nihil Obstat:
Rev. Adam D. Schmitt
Censor Librorum

Imprimatur:
✠Leo A. Pursley, D.D.
Bishop of Fort Wayne-South Bend
June 8, 1976

ISBN: 0-87973-801-4

Library of Congress Catalog Card Number 76-23698

Cover Design by Eric Nesheim

Published, printed and bound in the U.S.A. by
Our Sunday Visitor, Inc.
Noll Plaza,
Huntington, Indiana 46750

801

To Philip Scharper and Sally —
For Special Reasons

SACRAMENTS in the NEW LITURGY

Contents

Part II:
Ritual of Prayers and Blessings

FOREWORD

In imaginative and practical fashion numerous contemporary priests have developed fresh programs to reach and teach confused Catholics. These pastoral programs make maximum use of the "teachable moments" — those special occasions in life when people approach the Church.

In the Archdiocese of Hartford, Father Bernard Killeen has labored zealously to develop detailed programs for reaching and influencing parents and children. Especially noteworthy have been his preparatory programs for Confirmation, with the involvement of parents, requirements for study and service to qualify for Confirmation, etc.

Any parish priest should benefit from the experiences and recommendations set down in this book. I commend Father Killeen for his priestly work and writing, and warmly recommend this book to all involved in sacramental preparation.

Most Reverend John F. Whealon
Archbishop of Hartford

March 29, 1976

Part I

Manual for Priests and Other Ministers of the Gospel

INTRODUCTION

In his introduction to the Decree on the Sacred Liturgy from Vatican II, Father Clement J. McNaspy, S.J., rather casually makes this statement: "It was no accident that the Fathers of the Second Vatican Council took under consideration first, before anything else, the Liturgy." Even before the Council was adjourned many liturgical commissions here and abroad, undertook the renewal of the praying Church with great zeal and enterprise. It was apparent to many priests and ministers of the Gospel that there was a great source of spiritual wealth hidden in these new rites and prayers. Many of us made use of them to help our people in their efforts to create a real, practical renewal in the Church in the modern world. Sad to say, many well-intentioned efforts were lacking in the application of the practical and precise theme of the Council: Personalism — the fact that the Church is actually, practically concerned with each family and each person in each family of the Church.

From the beginning, the Liturgy — whether it was at the time of death or birth, of marriage or even confirmation — has always been a potential "teachable moment" of life, a time to demonstrate the unique love the Church has for her people. Prior to the loud pronouncement of the Second Vatican Council, we experienced a great deal of difficulty in showing this basic theme. Many priests were successful using the Liturgy of the Sacraments as a device, if you will, to grow closer to their people and to help their people to feel the Church's concern and care. By and large, simply by dint of custom and circumstances, the contrary attitude was much in vogue. Attitudes and practices in the old Church were verbalized so often in the old cliché "get 'em in — get 'em out." The response on the part of the people was in kind: "They don't know I'm alive" — or worse: "They don't care."

Now with the new rites and prayers available to us, I think, I know, we have an unlimited opportunity to correct these distortions and to develop this basic theme of Personalism in the Now Church.

Now is the time for us to show the world the true mission of the Church. The Fathers of the Council, in addition to their plea for Personalism in the prayer life of the Church, pleaded for the universal application of the principles of subsidiarity and collegiality. The plea of the Fathers must be heard and answered. For too long now have our people been confused, fatigued and even angered at some of the problems of the Church in the modern world. If we can show them the real working and praying Church in the light of these principles, we will do a good thing.

At important times in the lives of our people, when the liturgy itself is so sensitive to their needs and wants, we can do this with a little care, ease and profit — profit for them, ourselves and our communities. The practical times of which we will be speaking in this text very often are so charged with potential for good that we cannot risk losing any of the benefits that I know can accrue to us as the Church family. Many of these critical times are, or become, real "Moments of Truth" for our people — the gesture of Personalism on the part of the Church

14

occasions and almost demands a response from them — and the response can take the form of the total family commitment to God and Church, of which we will have much to say.

The text that I am offering to my fellow priests and ministers — and to some of our people who might profit from the experience of their fellow Christians, contains outlines of programs to be executed at the important occasions in the lives of the people. I have used these several programs over the course of many years since the close of the Second Vatican Council. I have found all of them to be most productive and practical and I would share this experience with others.

The first situation under consideration will be that of the time of death in our family — in any family in our community, with some mention of children in their real crises at the time of death at home.

We will proceed to a discussion of the Liturgies of Baptism, First Communion (with a brief review of the practical implication of First Confession), and Confirmation. A short note on Marriage will terminate our considerations. All the occasions provide exceptionally attractive challenges to priests and people. Hopefully, the programs will prove to be both attractive and adaptable to many in their ministry for the people in these times of distinction.

The diverse and multiple situations seem to me to provide for a realistic opportunity for priests and ministers for an increase and renewal of our own true priestly identity, present with the people, living, suffering, loving with them. With all due respect to the valid call for concern in our ministry for many social and political items of peace and reconciliation, these times of joy and sorrow give the vital qualities and characteristics of our ministry a realistic and vivifying thrust and support. The moments of (personal) mediation that accompany the person in his ministerial role at this time are of immense personal gratification and realistic humility. This may be a secondary consequence of any of the programs, but it is truly a valid one.

Of the essence in any of the programs is the controlling interest we have in the persons involved: that they are able to know and feel and understand precisely how important each is as an individual person or family in God's family — the Church.

A final item is the broader dimensions involved with regard to the community at large: the infectious nature of this good mentality — the Church cares about all of us, and this in the face of any bad feelings we have, or how hurt any one of us may have been in the past.

Throughout this text we will have repeated references to a total commitment to God and the Church by individuals or by entire families. We will be expecting the different "teachable moments" to be repeated occasions for this response on the part of the people. They will detect the warmth of the Now Church; they will understand the great respecter of privacy the Now Church is. They will observe the Now Church in a totality of concern for them that will be exciting, challenging and productive for all concerned.

As a final note, I would like to call the attention of the reader to the adaptability of the parts of each program. Some part of one idea may be suitable for a particular situation that we may face. Other parts of any one program may have to be substituted for another. We trust that all the programs as well as each part of them will bring about our object, that is a total family commitment to God and Church by our people.

16

1/ DEATH

On the day of the death of a member of God's family, I have found that the mere presence of the priest in the home of the family is a most vivid sign of the Church's concern for all her people. When a family is met with the stark reality that someone close to it has been called to his or her eternal reward, the Church through her priest can provide more comfort, by his office and his person, than any other person or sentiment can, normally speaking.

The family of the deceased is living through a day of extreme trial, psychologically and spiritually. The special circumstance of a particular case periodically alters the situation but usually the day upon which the person dies is the key day its members will always remember — it is the day on which they felt the shock the most — the time they need the care and cure that only their priest or minister can bring them.

I am starting this manual with a cursory outline of the several points that are important to us in our ministration to these people who need us. Some of the items

17

mentioned may not be applicable in every case or in some special case, but I do think each part of the plan will provide a real opportunity to demonstrate the theme of personalism in our Church.

There is no question that there are any number of distractions and practical difficulties which often impede and even prohibit our best intentions to help our people — even at this most critical time. So many times, when a mortician calls us to notify us of a death in the parish, our thoughts have been, and necessarily so, "Do we have a wedding scheduled?" "The snow is deep in that part of the cemetery." "I have other people in the office," etc. But the call for help from the family of the deceased is so desperate that nothing should keep us from it that very day — even if it has to be rather late that day. All other considerations must give way to this occasion for our demonstration of personalism to this family.

For the most part we become acquainted with the fact that a death has occurred in the parish through a call from a mortician. The family has already gone through the preliminary and practical arrangements that have to be made for the funeral. Once in a while we are able to be with family members, in the hospital or convalescent home or at the scene of an accident. But not very often. Even if we are there at the time of death, we can't effect the results that we expect from our conference with them at that time. Once they have finished with their doctors and the undertaker they are ready for us — to help them pray and meditate.

Where this conference takes place depends on the particular situation: either in their own home — especially if fatigue and grief make it necessary; or in church, if coming directly to God's house will help ease their pain; in the office of the rectory; in the funeral parlor — wherever is best, for privacy and for intimate discussion.

It is possible but unlikely that the survivors will not be able to pray and meditate at this particular time. In such cases, our conference could be postponed until the next day. By doing so we risk quite a bit. They probably will not sleep much anyway that night without medication, but our conference can give them a great deal of comfort that will aid them immediately.

When we keep in mind the purpose of our conference with these people we can be demonstrative in our concern for them and, at the same time, guarantee them the sacred privacy that they need at this time. We are with them to pray. We are there to help them in their meditation on the mysteries of life and death, exemplified by the deceased. The deceased may have been a very prominent sign of God's love among us, a person of faith and commitment to God and family, or he or she may not have been precisely that. It matters not. We can listen to the family tell of the goodness found in every person, that the deceased exemplified. We want to know. We have to know who this person was and what part he or she played in God's plan for His community. This may have been a deep mystery to all but it gives everyone something to think about, and remember.

A second point in our prayer with the family is the time of the person's death. This is almost a universal question: "When did he die? How old was he?" This is the quest of the human spirit: the why about the when of a person's death. Was there any significance as to the time of day or the day of the week or month in his life or in the family's? Is there any special reference to the place or circumstances of the person's death to be noted? Many of these considerations may not have very much

19

bearing on our understanding of the mystery of death, but then again they may.

A third personal point is the way the deceased approached the fact that he or she was going to die. In the life of the deceased this may have been a private dialogue with God. It may have been common knowledge. The fact that he or she is dead now warrants a thought about the family's and the community's preparation for the inevitable. The grief that we experience at the death of one close to us puts us in an emotional and spiritual tautness that is not present every day. We must capitalize on it to help us realistically renew our faith in the Resurrection of Jesus Christ and the mystery of eternal realism.

The preceding points of meditation will aptly serve to set the stage for the real purpose of the priest's visit. Part Two of this book, a ritual, contains a few short prayers and blessings the priest can say for and with the bereaved. This official gesture on the part of the priest should relax his people and enable them with comfort and humility to use any other suggestions and aids he might have for them. He will be able to strengthen them in their weakness and exhort them to carry this cross that they have with dignity and hope. He may have to soothe their anger at this time. He will certainly have to offer any guidance they may need because of the normal confusion that often follows the sudden death of a member of the family.

Most important at this moment is the gesture that the priest can make in offering his people the opportunity to receive the Sacraments of Confession and/or Holy Communion. The Sacraments will provide any needed help where some misunderstanding or resentment might exist or be envisioned among the different survivors. The

Sacraments will be an instrument of peace and reconciliation for all concerned.

When the members of the family at this time are given the opportunity to receive Holy Communion under these circumstances, they then truly, personally understand the words of the Savior: "Come to Me you who are heavily burdened — I will refresh you." Many times when they receive the Eucharist their faces will be wet with tears and their bodies racked with emotional fatigue. The presence of Christ with them and in them will bring the peace of soul they need. The final blessing of the priest will complete and conclude the rite.

Depending on the circumstances, the priest can use this occasion to outline with the family the Liturgy of the Mass of the Resurrection, an office that is suited to both priest and people at this time. This liturgical exercise: the selection of the Scripture readings, hymns and prayers as well as the appointment of any particular persons to be formally involved in the liturgy: concelebrants, lectors, etc., becomes a quieting, practical distraction from any disturbing pain or sorrow in the minds and hearts of the people. It is a return to the practical realities of life, while still surrounded by the tone of death. Life does go on for the rest of us.

This pastoral visitation with his people ought to be brief. The people are in need of some moments of private prayer and mourning. The priest can do all he has to do without much delay. He will find that he himself has much to think about on his swift return to the rectory about his place among his people and how they respond to his presence as the sign of the consoling and suffering Church and the symbol of faith in the Resurrection.

It well suits our purpose to demonstrate the personalism of our Church if the priest can spend a moment with a bereaved family on the day after the burial of a loved one. On this day, after the shock of the fact of the death has, as it were, worn off somewhat, the house is filled with a vague emptiness, as are often the hearts of the people involved. Their faith may well have generated a certain holy, peaceful resignation to the will of God but the simple presence of the priest with them for a blessing, a prayer, a brief meditation on God's love, sharing again their moment of lonesomeness — will help a great deal as each day goes by. There with them again the priest will be a reaching out of God's whole family to help the people to carry the weight of this sorrow.

It is impossible to calculate the effect that this gesture on the part of the priest will have on himself or on the community at large. Very often, the most pedestrian of gestures on the part of the Church can have far-reaching effects in the hearts of all the people. This simple visit at this time, very quietly, can show all the people a spiritual warmness and concern that they understand and appreciate. They detect and almost project how well they will be cared for in their own future moments of pain or trouble. It is not a security blanket but it is a comfortable community atmosphere.

Every pastoral activity can and should be an opportunity for our own spiritual development but there is none more charged with potential than this practical detail of being with our people at the time of death. Realistically, we preach: "It is appointed: to die." With our priestly people our faith is constantly refreshed with this fact, as we aid them in their effort to cope, in this world, with the eternal truth and the temporal reality of death.

It is with a great deal of hesitation and decision that I include the following notes in this manual with regard to death and children. How can we help the young to under-

22

stand, however slightly, and to react to the death of someone close to them? We have all experienced, with a great deal of uncertainty and trepidation, the situation where children had to be told of the death of a parent, grandparent or even another child. We sense beforehand the severe limitations that any such case presents, apart from any particular considerations. Yet, if we need all the help we can get from prophets, poets and priests in our attempts to understand death, we can see the desperate need children have.

The situation becomes more difficult for us, and more taxing, when we know that there is no set of ready answers that covers every case. Perhaps herein lies a clue to the best procedure. We are attempting to make the principle of personalism be more effective in our Church. The many variables that must be considered will challenge any person in his role of comforter of the afflicted child. Variables are the age of the child; the circumstances of the death of the deceased, whether by sickness or accident; the personal relationship the child had with the deceased; the spiritual encounters the child has experienced; any appreciation of God as a loving Being; the reaction of the peer group to this special situation. All these factors will determine the precise tactics that must be employed. They will demand our personal study of and attention to this child. Our approach is absolutely personal. No child will react in precisely the same way. We must be cautious not to say too much or too little. The prayers that we can say with them and the blessings that we give them will clearly illustrate our concern for them. This special gesture of tenderness toward the children will at least show them that we understand their problem. We are aware of their confusion. This in itself will support them in their lonesomeness. It will open up for them a channel of communication through which they can direct their questions and feelings. Only by this procedure can we find out the problems they are facing in the situation. It is the task of the priest, with many others of the family and community, professional and non-professional, to be ready to respond to the needs of the child, no matter what they may be. Perhaps with all so concerned, the children will weather the storm in which they find themselves.

2/ BAPTISM

If ever a death in the community is an auspicious occasion to illustrate and expedite the principles of personalism and collegiality given by the Council Fathers, the birth and Baptism of a new baby in our family is even more suitable. Father Joseph E. Payne, C.S.C., in the introduction to his text *Together At Baptism* very briefly gives a few of the ideas and ideals that can be used by the parents of the child to be baptized, the priest whose role it is to be the child's spiritual father, the godparents and the community at large. His text, though, is basically a ritual — and a good one. His brisk commentary supplies the people with many points for discussion and meditation. It can well serve the new parents and even the godparents as a prayer book during the early months of the child's development. And, if used to its ultimate purpose, can very efficiently dispose the family for the subject we are about to discuss: total commitment to God, and His family, the Church — and maybe, even more specifically, to the parish to which it belongs. I think this "Total Commitment" of which we will write must include the three items: time, talent and tithe. Father Payne mentions the concept of "Church as Community" and this can be our entré to the couple with the new baby; the new role that is theirs now in the parish community, involving their commitment.

Consider the case of a young couple where the new baby is the first child. In so many cases, even with the very good young Christian families, the concept of parish community or family is seldom appreciated. Up to now they have been privately engaged in so many serious things in their lives that they had neither the time nor the inclination to be members of the Church as a family. Many have been in school where their parish was at best a casual or fluid community with little or no stability. Their association with the priest was at times far from the normal father/son/daughter relationship. It could not even qualify for the term family. Often the chaplains at our universities and colleges are classified by the young people as just another part of the school administration. No matter how inventive many of our school priests have been, no matter how dedicated they were and are in their zeal to help the students, the very structure within which they operate makes it almost impossible for our young people to sense the concept of "Church as Community."

Love makes community, but young people have not experienced the love of the Church up to this time to any great extent. For the most part they have not lived with joys or sorrows long enough. They simply do not know life and its required love from others, outside their parents or immediate family.

There is another further complication. These young people are intent on their status and purpose as students. They are after an education. Their intellectual and emotional driving forces insist that distractions be dismissed

26

from their lives. Whether we like to admit it or not their religious life can become precisely that: a distraction, an interruption in their large plan. Many times they are so pathetically young in their spiritual and emotional lives, they cannot depend on the themes they hear from the parents or their priests: "Be sure to go to Mass and receive Holy Communion. Talk to the chaplain. Say your prayers." They have heard all this, time and time again, for years since they were little children. To hear it again at this time is just another monotonous noise in the background and they have no intention of giving it more than a casual ear.

A further obstacle to their ability to make a real commitment to their Church is the social and economic status they maintain as students. The chance to make new and varied social encounters occupies all the free time they can get or take from study. Naturally, this inclination to enhance their personal social position is regarded as a very real need. All this is certainly understandable but it must be noted as an occasion for the postponement of any real religious commitment. (Something could be said here in regard to the present status of vocations to the religious life in our country. The above item, it seems to me, is a part of our problem, but I shall delay the discussion for a while.)

Finally, we must note that many of our young people have detected in our modern Church a disturbing influence. Some of the unrest they exhibit is only a replay of the problems that have beset their elders, both at home and in church. It is no wonder they are more than a bit reluctant about casting their lot with us. Some of their complaints are simply the age-old chorus of young people expressing their rash and often wild enthusiasm to change everything that their elders did. Nonetheless, it provides another source of pain for them and further delays any possibility of their making their commitment to God and His Church.

Here is a special case: where the baby's father had been in military service. This applies in a most special way if they, the parents, were married during that time. While these men, and the women too, if they themselves were members of the armed forces, were in basic training, they looked upon the chaplain as just one more member of the staff whose role was anything else but a "father" to them. The chaplain is just like the doctor or the lawyer. "If you get into trouble, he can be of some help," but that is about it. After they leave their basic training the situation often becomes worse. They usually do not have to come in contact with the chaplain at all. If they were already married, their position in that Church was vague. They feel very little need of closeness to the Church family at the base or camp. They have their private social and economic ideas and pragmatics to develop and they can see no real benefit to be garnered from the Church in this area. So it is that in so many cases, these extraneous forces have delayed or even prohibited the total family commitment to the Church during this time, i.e., before its members are settled with real estate, job, friends, etc.

The first real occasion for an invitation to become a permanent part of God's Church family presents itself when they are waiting for the birth of their first (or even second or third) child. With all the factors that have influenced the young couple in mind, the next step rests with the other people in the Church to be as gracious and loving as they can be with the extension of this invitation. Sometimes this role will be directly that of the priest or minister. Many times he alone can function in this role at this time. He alone can demonstrate the mentality of the "good shepherd" looking for and finding these members of the flock who need his tender kindness to help them. Surely others in the Church can and should be of great help to him in many ways: knowing and caring about the expected birth of the baby, calling this fact to the attention of the priest or minister, with all due respect to privacy; by their prayer and concern giving subsidiary help to the expecting parents, etc. Let us not forget the role that professional people in the community should play in this whole enterprise, the enterprise of the community. The precise form that the invitation to the young couple takes will naturally be dependent on the judgment of the priest and the peculiar mentality of the couple. Again, from the beginning, the principle of personalism is of prime importance at this time. The priest or minister might bear in mind for his own effectiveness (and private spiritual advancement) this thought. Just as he is going out of his way to help any young couple, he must know and feel that his people, other priests and the laity would do the same for him in any time of difficulty he might have.

It is essential that the young parents understand that we don't care what happened in the past. All the problems they may have had with the Church or with themselves or with their families or with life in general are forgotten, dissolved or at least pushed aside right now. Today, "we are concerned with both of you personally and your new baby. Nothing else matters except that at this time you and your child get the VIP treatment you need and deserve." With this mentality clearly demonstrated to the people in an honest, sincere way the priest can proceed in the fashion he has determined will be best for this particular couple.

In each individual case, this mentality is absolutely essential. What worked for one, may not work for another. At all costs, we must avoid even thinking, much less voicing this normal but dangerous mentality: "Why can't these people do like everybody else? Who do they think they are? Why can't they get in line?" We must be very careful.

Personally, I have found that by way of prelude to the whole plan, giving a blessing to the mother, father and the house is the best way to get started. It sets the tone. I have found that no matter how many objections they may have, no matter how many problems they may be facing, no matter how antagonistic they may be toward the Church, the fact that the priest is willing and anxious to bless them, relaxes them and immediately enhances the chances of effecting the whole process. For this reason I have included in the ritual a special blessing for mother, father and the house, apartment, home.

After the blessing, comes the questionnaire. Note that the following questionnaire is meant to be rather universal. The hope is that all situations can be covered. Yet it is particular and adjustable. All problems can be aired. All objections can be heard. It is not the purpose of the questionnaire to pry, anymore than we have to. The sacredness of the couple's privacy must be maintained. We ought to make certain the spouses know why we are asking the questions, and this may take some explaining. We ought to ask only questions that are necessary to help them meditate on and resolve any obstacle to their accepting our invitation to commitment. Once one is successful in receiving a commitment from the parents of the child he may proceed to catechesis. If there is no real success at this particular time, one ought not to be overly concerned. There will be other occasions for it.

The catechesis is much more than a simple instruction. It should assume the form of a large plan of projected spirituality for this couple. The variations are without limit and can be geared to any level of intelligence, scholastic training or social background. Again we note the business of personalism. Herein lies the latitude of the total program including the possibility of simplicity in an explanation of the parts of the ritual. One of the problems and strong objections we have faced in the Church is that our liturgy and our explanations thereof have been for an elite corps of our people. This charge has been and is specious. The plan that we are discussing is absolutely adjustable to any person but it has to be fitted to every individual couple by the priest or minister.

I think the first item to be made clear in the mind of the couple is the fact that the Fathers of the Council insisted that everybody pay attention to the fact that the birth of this new baby is a sign and symbol of God's love in our community and it is to be shared by all. It must be prepared for by everybody, not just by the pregnant wife and working husband. This again presents the chance to demonstrate the idea of God's Church family. This baby's two-fold birth: physical and spiritual, is a public affair, over and above the simple recording by the registrar and the parish secretary of vital statistics. It demands the notice and concern of the whole family. A small item like this may well help the whole country to rupture much of the impersonalism in business, industry, politics and even in our smallest neighborhoods and parishes. This, of course, is a side benefit. Our primary concern is that the baby's parents feel the benefit of this directive by the Church. They should be advised of the prayers and love that accompany their vigil during the last weeks of the pregnancy. Ordinarily, this emotional

31

and spiritual support will simply make the couple feel more comfortable. But once in a while the absence of the father by reason of sickness, death, work, etc., or where there are problems: psychological, obstetrical, physical or financial, the support of the Church family can mean a great deal. It can be the way that serious problems and real harm to parents and child can be avoided. The large question of separation and/or lonesomeness is of prime concern at this particular point. This item is possibly of more importance in the case of the child's father, who might be away at school or on a business assignment or have some other reason for being away.

All that I have said is preliminary to a discussion of the different and complementary roles of the people involved in this baby's coming into the world.

The following questionnaire is presented as a guideline to help the priest determine the mentality of the people with whom he is working. Naturally, the most important people are the parents of the new baby, but the rest of the people involved very definitely have an impact on the case, so their feelings about the Church family ought to be investigated. They too must profit from this new baby's role in the Church.

The questions to be asked, naturally, cover quite a bit of ground. For many people, very few need to be asked. For some, all of the questions will reveal or lead into objections that must be answered or problems that must be discussed. This is the essence of the idea: to enable the people to honestly appraise their spiritual thinking and make accurate judgments and plans accordingly. We can help by asking questions in a gentle manner.

• **Questionnaire**
Has your life been too busy these past few years?

Have you had the time to study your role in the updated Church?

Have you experienced theoretical or personal doubts or problems in the updated Church?

Were you able to ask for help or get it when these problems upset you? Was it too much trouble to ask for answers or help?

Has your life as a married couple been close to the Church?

Have you been able to go to church every Sunday and receive the Eucharist?

Was there anything that happened to make you feel uncomfortable:

Your own strangeness in your adult life in the Church?

Your own dislikes of the people in the Church or of the rules in the Church?

Your own awkwardness in adjusting to the now Church?

Was it someone else's fault: A priest's, his personality or mentality? other parishioners?

Have your parents contributed in these past few years to your spiritual life? For better or worse? By advice or example? By intrusion or by total neglect?

What of your social group? Do these people help or hinder?

What of your neighbors? What of other members of the parish?

Do you think the birth of this baby will change your mind — or the way you've lived your spiritual life? For better or worse?

Do you look on this baby as a minister of God who will help you to be better Christians?

Do you believe that everybody, even the baby, has a

part to play in helping one another to be holy and comfortable and in getting to Heaven?

Will you be able to depend on the baby's godparents?

Do you believe that the role of a godparent is one of total interest and concern for the child, and not simply a substitute in the child's spiritual growth, to be demonstrated often both socially and economically?

What kind of a guarantee can you expect from the godparents in aiding in the sacramental growth of the child?

Are you prepared now, before this baby is born, to make a new pledge of your married life and love to God and the Church? Have you reviewed your wedding liturgy?

Are you willing to become a real Christian family at this time?

Do you realize how critical your decision is at this time?

Have either one or both of you had to make a decision like this before in your life?

Did anyone help you to do it?

What were the problems you met in making the decision?

What made you change?

In his introduction to the Decree on the Church (*Lumen Gentium*) Father Avery Dulles, S.J., observes:

> "Instead of beginning with a discussion of the structures and government of the Church . . . the constitution starts with the notion of the Church as a people to whom God communicates Himself in love. This provides an excellent foundation for a new and creative approach to the role of the laity in the Church."

The occasion of a child's Baptism brings this new appreciation of roles to the forefront and in his explanation of these, the priest will not only enhance the parents' commitment but will establish further grounds for relaxed comfort in their commitment and might even provide a new challenge for them in the Church. An outline of the distinct role each one of the participants plays will help one to appreciate the total effort that can and must be made. Subsidiarity works here very well. The new or at least resurrected view of the priest in the Baptism of the new baby must be explained to the parents. For many priests prior to Vatican II, and even for some presently, the administration of the Sacrament of Baptism was and is a routine chore to be expedited as rapidly as possible without any personal involvement with the parents or the family of the child. This was not due to any lack of zeal on the part of the priest for God's people. It was simply the routine, mimeograph system under which we labored. The Second Vatican Council changed all that and we priests now have the strong suggestion from the Church to be involved very deeply with these people. This new approach must be explained to the expecting parents. I think the first idea might well be to show the real connection between the Sacrament of Holy Orders and Matrimony.

The very title that the people use for priests is indicative of the real connection between the Sacraments. No other title we have — Reverend, Pastor, Right Reverend, etc. — expresses so neatly our relationship with the people. We are called "Father" by everybody and by this very fact, our role, however obscured in their minds, is established.

This title signifies an appointment by God to be a total father, at all times concerned with His children in matters of life on this earth, as well as in Heaven. Herein lies the heart of the matter. The couple must feel this idea. They must meditate on it, dwell on it. We must explain the meaning of "the bridge builder," the meaning of the priest as creator with regards to the new baby. He is the nourisher throughout the life of the child. This is not the time for a sermon to the young couple on the ministry of the priest but it will give them a more realistic view of the role of the priest in the Church and in this Baptism. It will emphasize the tone of personalism in the Church today and give an insight into their own role. Before we go into their role, we might mention the fact that one very serious feature of their role will be a sharing of the priesthood of the baptizing priest — so well brought out in the first gesture of the priest when he makes the sign of the cross on the baby's head and invites the parents to do likewise.

The posture of the people at the ceremony of the Baptism of the child gives a striking portrait of the role of the parents. The quasi-liturgical requirement and certainly the pastoral directive that both parents be present at the Baptism indicates the zeal of the now Church to illustrate the roles of both mother and father. This very idea will be the theme of the discussion the priest has with them in his catechesis. Too often in the past, there has been an overemphasis on the distinction of roles. While this distinction is valid, at times essential, it seems to me now there must be a real thought process on the part of the parents in their joint roles. Too often have we seen a dereliction of duty on the part of some men, expressed by the age-old refrain "she bore my son, she feeds my children, she teaches them their prayers." This is practical heresy and now is the time to nip it. They are both creators together with God. This child is the gift of God through their consecrated sexuality. The child's gesta-tion, aside from purely obstetrical considerations, has been good or bad, depending on whether or not husband and wife are both feeling good spiritually. If one does not "feel good" one is not going to live and/or work well. Good emotions are very essential at this time. The sacred encounter of their marriage, carried on day by day, their love and sacrifice every day, will be manifest-ed and blessed by God on the day of the child's birth and Baptism. How true rings out the final blessing of the priest at their wedding: "May you be blessed in your work and enjoy its fruit."

The parents are providers and examples of faith, leaders in prayer for their child. The list is almost with-out end and it will be the office of the priest to start them on their daily prayer and meditation. This item will be treated later on in the chapter. I want to conclude the dis-cussion of their role now and after the birth and Baptism of the child. This family needs a heart and it needs a head. Both are equally important. They must function together in harmony.

Very important at this point in the dialogue with the parents is the mentality they have in selecting the god-parents of their child. Many times there will be almost no need of any real discussion. They will understand very well their own role and will appreciate the added empha-sis the Church is placing on the subsidiary and collegial support the godparents are expected to supply. We have seen too often the case where strictly social factors de-termined the choice of persons to be godparents and, at times, not the very best social factors. In one notorious case, a person under indictment for "assault with intent to murder," was asked to be a sponsor. This custom must be altered. The responsibility of the godparent is tersely and directly discussed by the priest at the very opening of the ritual. During the interview it should also be explained. After the role of the parents is clearly discussed and defined, the priest can be of real help to them in selecting and instructing the godparents. One can never invade essential privacy, but with a modicum of manners, it can be effected. One would hope that the godparents could spend some time in dialogue with both the priest and the parents of the baby. This would, indeed, make for a total preparation — one in which everyone involved could be said to be totally committed to God, His Church and the proposition that the new baby will be well cared for by everyone in his or her family.

Here is a special note on the roles for grandparents. It is perfectly obvious in the official ritual for Baptism that the Church has retained, for excellent reasons, many items that have been used for centuries in the Church. I see in the role of grandparents an excellent opportunity for them to be agents of restoring or at least capitalizing on many ethnic and cultural customs that have gone out of vogue in our modern Church life. These grandparents ought to be encouraged and directed to pursue this special vocation with vigor. Some have been reluctant, as they would put it, to intrude at this time, in the lives of their children, not wanting to be old-fashioned. With dexterity and propriety they can contribute immensely to the preparation of the birth and Baptism of their grandchild. Each case naturally rests on its individual merit. Some will have neither dexterity nor propriety. Many will. We will list here only a few contributions. Again the list is almost without limit:

Songs and poems of the family, plus stories;
Songs and poems of the country of origin;
Prayers, both public and private;

Stories about the baptismal robe as well as the baptismal candle.

A great deal more could be said on this subject. The final chapter of this manual has more than is stated here.

In the case of the Baptism of a child when he or she is not the first child, we have a few items that concern any older child or children on the occasion of the birth and Baptism of the new baby. We will not mention the emotional and/or psychological "sibling rivalries" that may or may not occur, although the spiritual preparation and the role the older child will play at the birth and Baptism may well be of some help in these other necessary preparations. Noting that we are engaged in total family commitment, it is never too early to allow a child or children to become familiar with the little but real role they can play.

Looking first at any preschool child, the controlling interest is one of celebration. The birth and Baptism are prepared for as for any big party. Every day must have some small notice as the time for the birth approaches, so that everyone will be excited and joyful. The celebration should start quietly, several days before mother goes to the hospital. Her absence from the home will be part of the celebration and excitement. The return of mother and baby will allow the child to rejoice and celebrate in concert with mother, father and the new baby. The celebration every day and the big celebration with father, the priest, the new baby, parents, etc., will be in God's house — then home for another party.

During the course of helping the child to understand his/her role and balance or neutralize any misgivings, hidden or overt, the child can be given a history of his or her own Baptism, complete with pictures of his/her celebration when he/she was born. Further, if the child is old

39

enough, and actually age four is quite old enough, he or she will participate in the baptismal ceremony itself. For this a little rehearsal should be conducted. This will give the father of the new baby a fine opportunity to illustrate the sharing of roles by priests and parents. In simplicity, the parts of the ritual can be explained and further excite and satisfy the normal curiosity of the child. One caution: all reference to sin, washing away dirt, etc., must be avoided at all costs, for obvious reasons. This child is preparing for a beautiful party of a beautiful clean baby. The child's role is to help bless the baby with God, the priest and the rest of the family.

Another further dimension is in the case of older children, those who have already made their First Communion. They know celebration, Church celebration. They have encountered their Church family. Already they have communicated with Jesus. They know God's house. They know God is within us. They know God is at home, at the table, in their bedroom. They know Jesus loves them. "That's why He gave us a new baby." They still like celebration. They will certainly participate in the ceremony and, consequently, a more refined and detailed rehearsal is in order.

It seems to me the best way to stimulate and explain the role of older children, above age ten, is to give them a little quiz, and/or give them several projects. The quiz, of course, is a small study for the parents, to enable them to judge how knowledgeable the older child is with regard to birth and Baptism. This could well provide an excellent opportunity for sex education and development by both parents.

The quiz given, again with personalism, will demonstrate the concern of the Church family for the older child while the main emphasis is on the new baby.

- **Quiz**
  a. Do you remember when you were baptized?
  b. Who among your family does remember?
  c. Have they told you what happened?
  d. Now, you tell me what happened.
  e. How big were you?
  f. Did you have lots of hair?
  g. Will God be here when the baby comes?
  h. Where did you get your name?
  i. Who else has that name?
  j. Who was Saint _____?
  k. What kind of oil did the priest put on you? Where did he put it? Why did he do this?
  l. Who is the bishop?
  m. Who held you when the priest poured the water?
  n. What will you give the baby for his/her spiritual birthday?
  o. Why does the baby have to be baptized?
  p. Will it be fun?
  q. What will you do at the Baptism?

Nothing will help older children more than if they have to do something to help get ready for the new baby's birth and Baptism. The possibilities are unlimited. This ought to be left to the ingenuity of both parent and child. Just to mention a few: making a baptismal robe; making the baptismal candle; making banners for church and home; making a collage, or preparing a history of the family's participation in liturgical celebrations, Baptism, First Communion, etc.

We will finish this discussion of roles with a mention of the home. As remote as it may seem at first, when one just calls to mind how the "stable" of Bethlehem has been such a focal point for the commemoration of our

Lord's birth, the house — home — apartment of the new baby must have a similar role. We are, of course, not speaking of hospitals or lying-in-pavilions. That is quite another matter and should be discussed by hospital chaplains. Whether the home be a mansion, a high rise duplex, a cottage or a cold-water flat, this is where the life of the baby starts. This is where God's love came. It ought to look like a place where God's love, in the new child, is expected. Hence, the mother and father, knowing this, will appoint their home with significant artifacts. Nature, of course, will do its part. During the nine months, the very picture of trees, birds, sunrise will change and, as it were, develop as does the child *in utero*. So should the home.

A simple suggestion to the couple will open up to them new avenues of prayer. They have to be led to understand the fact that their family is the holy family and that their house is holy. They should make sure it looks holy. In addition to the crucifix, basic are figures of Our Lady and St. Joseph. I suggest that they carve or draw representations of a young, pregnant, beautiful Jewish girl and a strong male Hebrew, if they are able. If not, the market is flooded with any type they like. Again, the possibilities are unlimited. All we have to do is mention it. This we have to do. Then, let them take it from there.

The ritual has several blessings, not the least of which are the prenatal blessing and the blessing of the home.

There is almost no need to discuss the rite of Baptism as such because Father Payne has done such a great job in his text, *Together at Baptism*. His text is for the people. A small suggestion has been made by a presumably sophisticated minister of God that this manual ought to be presented to the people of God. It could be of some help to them. I will simply suggest a few items that are of concern to us. There is no better time to demonstrate the concepts of personalism and collegiality to the young couple, their friends, family and the community at large than at the actual Baptism. After having prepared themselves so well, after having thought and prayed over the promise and commitment they made to God and to each other, the ceremony itself fills them to capacity with holy euphoria. One can see the seriousness in the face of the young father. One can detect in the hands of the mother all the emotion that she has been through and is still experiencing.

The first question, "What have you named your child?" indicates immediately the personalism of the now Church. The child is not given a number but a person's name. Shortly after the Second Vatican Council adjourned, hagiography died. No publisher in this country would accept a manuscript about a saint — ancient or modern. Those books just would not sell. Now that many things have settled down, the people of God are buying. They are very interested in biographies. They want and they need this return to a long tradition in our Church. So, at this nomination of their child, comment should be made on the patron saint. There is no difficulty if the name is Peter or Mary but even if it is Ofo or Diana, there is room for comment. We are God's community in celebration and St. Ofo or St. Diana or whoever, is in heaven and all the family of the new baby should be reminded of this fact.

The welcome itself presents an interesting bit. There is no better way for the liturgy committee of the parish council to function than to be present at this precise moment. Even if there is no parish council as such, people of the parish, preferably those well known as members of

God's family, should be present. There will always be problems of schedules with which we must cope. The impact of the parishioners' physical presence at the ceremony is of such value to the Church at this time that nothing ought to interfere with it. If we must schedule them as we do our altar boys and ushers, so be it; it will be all worthwhile. It will, in fact, be the community in the person of man, woman, standing there with their priest and the new person in the community, the new baby.

The prayer of exorcism — either one given in the ritual is most interesting. The ideas of "rescue" and "freedom" convey, with strength, the mentality of temptations. This is no laughing matter, not something to be dealt with in novels and/or movies. The fact that satanism in the modern world is dismissed summarily as childish popery does not give us an excuse to do likewise. Any of us who have been in this world for any length of time are certainly aware of temptation. This baby will need more than just Baptism to get to heaven. The parents and everybody else must be reminded of this hard, cold fact. They do not need a dissertation, but a minute's reflection is needed.

A longer discussion concerning the oil of catechumens and of chrism will appear in Confirmation but it helps to show the people the oils. I have found that it is a fine time for them to be introduced to the idea that the bishop is our father in Christ and if he could, he would like to baptize every new baby. He cannot, but he sends us the holy oil that he himself blessed. Many are not aware of this fact but they should be. It is just one more opportunity to demonstrate the concept of the Church-family.

In Chapter VII, Number 129 of the *Decree on the*

Liturgy, the Fathers of the Second Vatican Council speak of "the suitability and dignity of the baptistry." The font itself, whether it be of stone, wood or plastic, has to say something to these people. We referred earlier to the home of the couple with the new baby and how it ought to be decorated. Comment ought to be made about the font, water and the shell. Almost anything at all will suffice, just as long as the new parents get the picture of what the Fathers of the Council mean in the above quote.

The dramatic renunciation of Satan and sin with the profession of faith by the parents and godparents of the child provide such a holy shock to the whole procedure that a good, rather long comment at this time is necessary. From one point of view, the very formality of the questions enables the parents to give voice to their deep spiritual feelings. Presumably, they have made their total commitment to God and the Church and now to voice it, just prior to their child's christening, enhances their joy and, at times, their new status in the Church. A holy pride is in their voices, pride in their love and pride in each other and so it is with the godparents. They know now that they are in a new Church. They know that they would not be allowed to take on this responsibility if they themselves were not real Christians. So the answers to the questions of the priest come back loud and clear. Their voices, with the chorus of the members of the parish, make for a real symphonic prayer to the Almighty. This is the time for a word of congratulation by the priest and the members of the parish council. Though it is not officially in the text of the ritual, it would not at all be ruled out of order to inject a "kiss of peace" into the proceedings in order that the people may share the strength and joy.

One final comment on the ritual. Though these blessings in the conclusion of the rite are short, as they should be, they are as beautiful as can be. This is the final item in the blend of the new and the old in the liturgy. Many young girls are not familiar with the Hebrew practice of purification. Though it was strictly symbolic and ceremonial, many of our people have never heard of the "churching of women," and a mention of this custom will help to make the blessings more meaningful to them. Of course, the blessing of the father ties everything neatly together and then God's blessing sends them forth.

If it is at all possible, the baptizing priest would do well to join the family for the social celebration which usually follows the liturgical celebration. The party will go on without him but even if he is only able to stop at the home for a few minutes, it will bring just that added joy to the couple who have had the baby, and to their family and friends. It may not seem to be much to us, but to them, especially if they have just joined the Church for good, it means a great deal. It relaxes them more to find their priest or minister coming to their home to break bread, as humble as the home and bread might be. They will remember this gesture. It will help them in the months ahead as they strive to prove their commitment.

One final item is some sort of "follow up." This situation must be worked out by individual priests and ministers according to their own particular situation and that of their families. The possibilities are varied. Some might prefer to again make a house call. This would be best — another little private meeting, or a casual review of the past few months. Others may decide to hold a conference at church, a para-liturgical session, bless the babies again; perhaps a lecture. I have found that the celebration of the Mass complete with another blessing of the child and mother and father is an exciting opportunity for several families in the community. It gives them a chance to see one another and, as it were, compare notes. Almost anything will do. It will show the parish and the new parents just how interested in them we are personally. They are not machines. They are people and we know it. We will care for them as such.

• **Conclusion**

When this total program for the care of souls, at the time of the birth and Baptism of a new baby, is viewed very objectively, I think the reader can see a great many possibilities for the different people with whom he works. Some features of the program may not appeal to every priest nor may some be that helpful to every parent. I do think that in every case we can be discerning enough so that every one of the couples can be shown our concern for them. They cannot resist any small demonstration of love and care we have for them at this time. They are especially attuned at this teachable moment in their lives to the Church's personalism, and we can certainly expect a response to this interest in their lives with this new child in the setting of God's family.

If we do the job tolerably well now when the child is born, we may not have to try nearly so hard later on in the child's life. This program for Baptism is designed not to make work for the priest but to reduce and refine it.

3/ FIRST CONFESSION

The occasion of a child making First Communion brings an added dividend to a family's spiritual treasury. The time is apt for both an introduction of the child to the whole concept of forgiveness and Penance, and also for the parents' investigation and/or review of their own mentality with regard to confession and the new order of Penance. We are talking here about the people who are committed to God and the Church.

For several years, there have been many interesting experiments carried on with regard to a child's First Confession — the time, the setting, etc. They have all been of value. They have served well as a fitting background for the Vatican declaration of May 24, 1973: "That these experiments . . . should cease and that everybody everywhere should conform to the Decree *Quam Singulari*." Before giving this directive, the Sacred Congregations refer to the *General Catechetical Directory*, in these words: "Having consulted episcopal conferences the Holy See believes that it is proper to continue the Church's custom of placing First Confession before First Communion." This is the mind of the Church. Given this mentality, we can most practically demonstrate our personal concern for the individual child and fit the celebration to his or her personal needs. The opportunity is here to expand the child's awareness of sin in the world and the essential forgiveness that it demands. They have to learn — they have to be taught — to be sorry. They have to learn, they have to be taught the concept of community and the effect sin and sorrow have upon it. There is no better time than now, at First Confession. The process of total education in this regard is long and gradual, but if it is started now and geared and fitted to the individual child, we will have made a good start.

When the parents present the child to the priest, both in a private interview and at a liturgical celebration, both advance in knowledge, solidarity and love. In our now Church, the child's preparation for Confession benefits his or her parents immensely. Change in religious practices comes hard to most people but our people have been most responsive to other liturgical changes and they are, and will be, in the matter of Confession also, once they understand and feel the benefits of a new approach to this mystery. We know that many have stopped going to Confession for all practical purposes. Others have never grown out of childhood habits and mentalities, some destructive to their spiritual peace, others harmful obstacles to their growth and maturity.

It is our task to discover any difficulties they may have and to provide guidance, direction and support in this time of spiritual growth. Our personal attention to their particular question or attitude will make this growth steady and secure.

Many other people in our Church have, in fact, looked to this encounter with new vision and new hope. They have made practical use of both the sacramental and consultatory graces available, to help them in their new life in the now Church. This is the time for any director of souls to channel their good will, to tax their ingenuity, to help them understand the treasure of God's grace for growth in their family spirituality. This is a magnificent opportunity for us, the ministers of God.

By way of review and conclusion, we may say that when at Baptism a real family commitment is established to God, and to His family, the Church, new relationships are established between priests and parents. Relationships are established then between parents and the large family, the parish. The parish takes on the role of "consultant." A personal relationship is established with their priest, whoever he is. This relationship is based on a familiarity, a confidence and a respect for the roles that each will play. There is also a delicate understanding that each one has. The role of the priest is not that of a pediatrician or nutrition expert or child psychologist. There is a certain understandable respect for privacy in many areas of normal family growth of the good home. As the family grows and develops, so do the roles develop — the role of the priest, the role of the parents and the role of the parishioners. Now at First Communion time, with these attitudes toward individual roles and family commitment rather well developed for some seven years, a new thrust is given. A new and stronger bond is given to priest, people and parents. This is important for the child making his First Holy Communion.

Let there be no mistake. At First Communion the roles have not changed. They have developed. There is still no switching of roles. They are not mixed up; they are not confused. The big plus is the fact that the child now comes into the total picture. The child assumes the role of contributor to the family, to the parish, to our group. He or she sees and understands the strong bond that exists between parents and the priest and the Church community. This is the basis for a further new and additional bond in the Church family of priest, parent, child and parish.

Underlying all of this is the growing and developing love at home and in the Church among all in God's family, flavored by trust and confidence. This formal respect and this warming love guarantees in the years ahead extremely fertile ground for growth by the whole family. During this time there will be multiple opportunities for a repeated renewal of individual and family commitment to each other and to the Church family. Finally, no one can possibly put a limit on any community's increased capacity for growth. All that we have said previously will guarantee the growth in God's love that we seek in the modern Church community.

4/ HOLY EUCHARIST

The parish priest is constantly aware of the different situations that present themselves in the total living of his parish family. The regular occurrences of death and birth present him with key moments in which to exemplify the Church's concern for the people. In the context of the total spiritual development of the parish and the community, the normal growth of each child presents many practical moments for judicious review and renewal of commitment on the part of the child's family. When the child is preparing for the reception of First Communion, the priest and the parents of the child can very efficiently blend their respective roles in the Church to enhance the good spiritual health of all concerned. When any one or several children receive this Sacrament, the priest has a unique opportunity, different from those moments presented at death or Baptism, to demonstrate to the child, to the family of the child and to the community, the deep significance of total family commitment to the Church. He can use the occasion to review for all the people the necessity of this commitment. He can demonstrate to them the far-reaching benefits which the commitment will bring to the whole community — with time and talent and, most practically, the tithe.

We will discuss in this chapter just how the priest can do this with efficiency and personal satisfaction. We will enjoy his teaching and giving as he demonstrates the principles of collegiality and subsidiarity in the now Church.

In the ritual we will include a few simple blessings which the priest can give to the child and the parents at this time.

The word "subsidiarity" is only mentioned in the decrees of the Second Vatican Council three times. We know, however, it is contained in essence in every single decree that it finds very practical usage in this Sacrament of First Holy Communion. We will discuss, first, the situation of a family in which the young people, at the time of their child's Baptism or even at their wedding, made a real total family commitment to God and the Church, and have kept the commitment with their child over these past seven or eight years. When the mother and father sense the thinking of the Church, that they have the primary responsibility of deciding when their child makes his First Holy Communion, they display a deep realization of how "subsidiarity" is working in the now Church. They know they are more competent to judge the emotional and religious development of their child than any priest, nun or religious coordinator. They are delighted to exercise their responsibility. The encouragement we give them at this time creates in their hearts and minds a further realization of the meaning of their Church family. They are more than willing to have all the help they can get from their priests and any parochial program that may be developed. They are energetic in developing private, personal programs of their own, carried on at home, which are designed for their own child's special talents and propensities. Often they are able to share their experiences with friends or neighbors. This is a significant contribution to the parish and community at large. It certainly makes them feel and act like the Church — the people living, working and loving God and helping each other to be better Christians.

As the child is preparing for the reception of First Holy Communion, the understanding of the concept of Church-family becomes refined and revitalized. For some time now, this child has been made aware of the Church by his parents' demonstration of closeness to God and other people in the Church. The child has been taught, both by the word and example of his parents, how comfortable it is to be joined to other people in God's family. The child, by merely living in this atmosphere, appreciates the closeness his family has with the priest, and the Sisters or teachers who instruct him. At the time of First Communion, when a conference is held between the parents and the priest, the child will become more and more convinced of just how important he or she is, personally and individually. Psychiatrists tell us that at this tender age, a great deal of emotional security is guaranteed simply by the attention given him or her by parents and priests. This, indeed, is a bonus that we can well use in the lives of these little ones.

A further item is to be noted. All the spiritual support the children are receiving at this time, eminently prepares them for their new status as communicants. They are no longer babies in the Church. They are children. They have a very definite role to play in the prayer and love life of the Church family. Just as their parents begin to operate more efficiently as the now Church, so will they. We must not neglect to mention here the added security that the child's obvious growth in stature brings to the mother and father of the child. They themselves need to be reassured of the accuracy of their commitment decision. The First Communion of their own child does precisely that. They can, with a great deal of self-satisfaction, participate in this event. It is the first of several "landmarks" that they will see as their married life and love grow. Finally, it gives them the energy to continue for the next seven, eight or nine years with greater confidence in themselves and their role in the Church. There is no more critical time in their lives as parents than the next several years. These years must be very productive for themselves and their children. Our special, individualized programs at this time will aid them immeasurably.

There is no real need for us to go into a detailed discussion of the programs that can be developed in any given locality. There are any number that can be worked out according to the practicalities of the given place. Just to mention a few briefly: Some contend that there is no need for the children themselves to have organized classes as such, that it is better if the parents are instructed by the priests or the Sisters and then the parents can instruct their own children. This has some merit. Others prefer to maintain a structured course for the children in conjunction with conferences and/or lectures for the parents — monthly or weekly — or whatever. It really does not matter how you do it, as long as the necessary "togetherness of purpose" is maintained. As long as the children know, and see that their priest and their parents and teachers are all involved in their First Communion, we are satisfied. Both parents must be involved, however, otherwise we defeat the theme of collegiality.

In the event there is no well-defined program in use, I shall outline one briefly. Again I trust it will be as adaptable to the varied circumstances that will be met as the program for Baptism was.

The first item of procedure is to hold a conference for all the parents of children who might be candidates for First Communion. It is essential that all members of the community — good, bad, and indifferent — have an opportunity to hear about, discuss and object to this new approach to the Sacrament. At this conference they are first advised of the themes: the collective responsibility all of us have in helping their child to prepare for the Sacrament; the primary capability they themselves have, and the secondary expertise that the priest and teachers have.

The second part of the program involves the main item of concern for parent and child during the course of study. The emphasis in this part of the program is the combined effort that parent and child will make together. Naturally, the subjects covered by any syllabus or textbook will provide both parent and child with liturgical and scriptural studies that will guarantee a well-rounded background for the coming advancement of the child.

The final item is the private conference or formal interview between priest, parents and child. Herein the power structure operates to capacity. The primary move made by parents to present the child to the priest, the acceptance of the candidate by the priest at the time judged proper and precise by the parents, the aptitude of the child for the Sacrament — all in concert — demonstrate collegiality and subsidiarity in action. This is our object. All have been taught, by their own experience at this time, the Church's personal concern for them and their child. It is at this moment that their total family commitment to the Church pays the dividend that was promised when they made it. The occasion demands a renewal of the commitment and it is very seldom refused.

Finally, it must be absolutely clear in everyone's mind that the responsibility of decision rests with the parents. They may consult, they may discuss and they may question the Sister or teacher of their child, and they must talk to the priest about their child; but they are the ones who are going to make the decision that their child is ready to receive First Communion.

A note can be made here with regard to the effect any or all of these programs can have on the community at large. Without going into any great detail, we know that the particular personal attention given to these candidates for First Communion, and their families, demonstrates time and again the concern of the now Church. It shows the mentality of the Church both in regard to collegiality and personalism. It is the office of everyone in the Church to make these ideals known to the whole world, despite the fact that many people of the community may not be directly involved with any one of the children receiving First Communion. They know what is going on and they share vicariously in the sense of belonging to the Church-family. This has the two-fold effect of reciprocal closeness in our Church for all the people, as well as for the family of the communicant. This closeness will provide an atmosphere of practical awareness in many other areas where personal interest and concern for each other can guarantee the truly God-like help that is so often needed in our daily efforts to live the Christian life, with all its practical problems.

With these facts in mind, the priest or minister will do well to advertise and publicize his program, just to guarantee the fact that everybody will know what is going on. The spirit of the people and the themes of the program will help to finalize the ideals of our now Church.

- **Holy Eucharist — A Commitment**

We have already posited the fact that the time in a child's life when he or she is ready intellectually, socially and emotionally to receive First Communion is a teachable moment of the highest rank. The occasion demands individual care and concern for each child and his or her family. This concern, almost of necessity, evokes some response in the form of commitment by the entire family. Problems do exist, however.

So in this section, in our treatment of the reception of First Communion by a child in our community, we must consider the case of the family which has no real family commitment to God or to the Church. The fact that there will always be some of our people who have not made any commitment at the time their child was baptized, should neither surprise us nor disturb us. The reasons for this are many and varied. A short discussion of them will help us to consider different strategies and tactics to use in our effort to help them, now at First Communion time, to make their commitment.

This teachable moment is a ripe occasion. It must not be allowed to pass without capitalizing on it. The very first case is the one in which nobody in the Church had the opportunity to invite the young couple to make a total family commitment when they had their first baby or, for that matter, the second or third child. Many times it was simply a matter of circumstances, a great variety of them. Sometimes, it was a simple matter of time and place. With the real shortage of clergymen of all kinds in our country, it is no surprise that the young couple had no one near them to make the contact that would have introduced them to this Christian way of life in modern society. It was no one's fault. It may have just happened that way. Other people may have been willing and ready to help but they just minded their own business. Consequently, the couple never really had the opportunity or the occasion to make a family commitment.

The situation is quite different where there was an opportunity to make a firm family commitment to God and to the Church but these people refused to make that commitment. The reasons why are many. The first is obvious: they thought there was no need to do this. They had the mentality and I shall phrase it in this fashion: "We got along so far very well. Why should we go all the way in this commitment business? We are happy as it is." The second reason is not quite like the first but it certainly follows normally right behind it. In this way we shall phrase it: "We like to be nominal Christians. Of course, we want to have the baby baptized. It's very nice. It's a very important social function. We believe in God, but believing in the Church, in other people, no thank you. We can get along by ourselves. We have done it so far and we will continue to do so. We don't need a lot of other people interfering in our personal, private affairs."

There is another whole series of cases where there exists some particular problem. The first is where there is no real faith in either mother or father. This situation is even more critical than the one mentioned above where the faith is weak. Here it is dead. The reason to have the baby baptized is simply to please somebody else — their parents or others in the family. This is an extremely difficult case with which to deal.

Another problem arises when parents have no trust in the Church. This lack of confidence may have come from a disagreement with the priest or minister. It may have come from a hostility toward other members of the parish community. It doesn't make any difference where the mentality comes from. These people are angry. They just want to get their child baptized without any real personal involvement.

There is a somewhat different but equally real excuse: the people have no real confidence in themselves or in each other. In some cases, there is very little solid evidence to hope that their marriage commitment will be fulfilled, and there are good reasons for trepidation. So, with the Baptism of the baby, neither is able, literally, no matter how tempting it might be, to make the commitment to the Church and to God. They cannot. They are just too uncertain of themselves.

Once in a while, we have a combination of all the aforementioned conditions. The parents, by themselves, would not even bother to have the child baptized, but they are under pressures from parents, family and friends to have the child baptized. They know full well they are being hypocrites. Yet, these pressures demand this social affair and/or quasi-political function. It has no bearing whatever on their religious thinking or practice. It is just something they have to do. There will be no thought of making any commitment for themselves or, for that matter, carrying out any plans for the child's future life as a Christian. Now the question is, what can we possibly do in such cases? Mentalities will vary with the individual client-person, but we know that a certain percentage of these people will wake up to the facts of life at the time of their child's First Communion. Often a simple invitation will effect this end — their understanding of the situation they are presently in, and the decision to make a feeble effort to change their lives. They may be prepared for this change immediately or they may be so reluctant to do it that it takes a year, two years, or even three, before they can bring themselves to make this most significant move to establish themselves with God and His Church. We must seize this opportunity to give them every chance in this world.

The following is a rather sketchy outline of some of the procedures one may use. The first thing to do is to make certain they know the difference between the old and the now Church. This takes time but, if it is explained to them, often this is enough to wipe out any objection. Any or all of their problems may stem from the impersonalism, legalism and authoritiarianism of the pre-Council Church. Others will come from their own lack of awareness of their real new status in the Church.

Once these items have been managed, one should investigate the presence of any real personal problem or objection they may have which could possibly keep them from making a real commitment now. Naturally, some of their objections or questions will be absolutely ridiculous. Most are baseless. To them they are real and we must treat them as such. If this is done, they might be able to make a real commitment, whereas they could not possibly have made it before. All this will require a great deal of patience and understanding on our part to answer all of their questions and objections. This is not time for us to dismiss or belittle. This may be their very last chance to take care of their family in the spiritual realm. Sometimes, they have never even considered all the benefits that can accrue from this commitment of which we speak. They need this fundamental responsibility to secure some psychological and spiritual comfort in the world we live in; they need it. They cannot depend on anyone else to guarantee their child's emotional and spiritual development. The time goes by very, very fast. Unless it is done now, the chances of its being accomplished sometime later are extremely slim.

Finally, we must make note of this. Everybody has a social responsibility to the other families in the community — especially to the other children. The creation of a spiritual atmosphere in the neighborhood and in the town is everbody's responsibility. No one can think that his influence is unimportant. If one family does not contribute to a wholesome, constructive tone in the community, they contribute to its destruction. They may not have understood or appreciated this fact until now. If so, now is the time to correct it. It does not take heroics; but we must be practical.

In conclusion let me note this. We dare not be reluctant to strongly urge, request or even demand, that they give the now updated Church a guarantee that they will start and continue to be in the Church and with the Church. It is absolutely out of the question to allow their child to receive First Holy Communion until they themselves are established with God and the Church. If they have to wait and think and pray for one or two or three years, so be it. If they can make up their minds to this proposition now, then they can and must forget about the past. We leave that to God's loving mercy. They must be reminded, however, that this is probably the last chance they will have. At the time of the child's Confirmation it will be probably be too late. That is, if the child ever gets to Confirmation. The odds are very much against it.

5/ CONFIRMATION

At the risk of being repetitious, I feel that it is necessary, before we start to discuss the Sacrament of Confirmation, to reiterate the theme of this manual. We stated in our introduction that we would discuss different practical, parochial programs that could be used in whole or in part to insure or renew, to establish or reestablish, a total commitment to God and the Church by our families. We trust that this theme will be evident throughout this chapter as we look at the Sacrament of Christian adulthood from many points of view.

In our modern Church there has been much experimentation in our efforts to make the reception of the Sacrament of Confirmation more meaningful to our young people and to their parents and peers. In our modern Church, there has been no greater need than to provide the young people with a much more sophisticated approach to this Sacrament of Christian adulthood. Our times call for new and dynamic approaches which will challenge our young people and encourage them in their maturing process. The program I will discuss has been used and found to be just that: a different and demanding structure that enables them — the recipients of the Sacrament — to move forward with a new vision and appreciation of their status in the Church. This program, as you will see, is not merely a structured syllabus for the candidates for the Sacrament. The program is an involved exercise in shared responsibility with the family of the candidate and the whole parish. It is a structured exercise in subsidiarity with responsibility shouldered primarily by the candidate and secondarily by his family and the parish. Naturally, the endeavor will involve a great deal of prayer, work and study by all concerned and will have its proportioned results — the rededication or commitment of the whole family to God and Church. This program contains a new dimension in the commitment that we have discussed in previous chapters. It involves the young candidate as a participant in the family commitment. It demands a new decision — a personal decision on the part of people who have never before had to do this in their lives. Heretofore their parents were responsible. Now they have an opportunity to be supportive in a real sense of the decisions their parents made long ago.

Before we outline the elements in this program, I quote the Fathers of the Council. Their words capture the theme of this program accurately. They said in the *Decree on the Apostolate of the Laity,* in Chapter three, paragraph 12: "Young persons exert very substantial influence on modern society. There has been a complete change in the circumstances of their lives, their mental attitudes and their relationships with their own family. Frequently, they move too quickly into new social and economic conditions. While their social and even their political importance is growing from day to day,

64

they seem to be unable to cope adequately with the new burdens imposed upon them. Adults ought to engage in friendly discussion with young people so that both groups can become better acquainted and share the special benefits each generation has to offer the other."

It strikes me that if the young persons in our Church are to have the influence on society and the Church that they should have, they must use the occasion of their reception of the Sacrament of Confirmation as their starting point. We, conversely, must use every device, every method, every program to equip them with the qualifications they need and the guidance necessary to function in this capacity. We hope this program for Confirmation will do just that.

Before we take an overview of the program, a few preliminary notes might be helpful. This program has more than one theme. We are primarily interested in preparing the candidate for the Sacrament, but we cannot do this without creating in the home and the community an attitude and an atmosphere that will be conducive to and supportive of our new approach to the Sacrament. Consequently, we have one program with involvement by several different people or groups of people.

This program demands a response on the part of the candidate and the family. This response can take the form of real, mature Christian commitment or it can result in a postponement of the reception of the Sacrament by reason of incompetency, immaturity or a general lack of understanding of the involvement the reception of the Sacrament implies. In either case, a moment of truth in Christian living is encountered.

The program, as it is offered, may be used in its entirety if it suits the immediate needs of any parish or its fulfillment may be viewed as a long-range objective, with parts of the program adopted as time goes on. The question of the proper or best age of the candidates will be discussed. It may take some years for the ideal to be reached in any community. The different parts of the program then become escalating phases to fill the stages of development until the candidates reach the proper chronological age.

This chapter is made up of two programs, one for the candidates and one for their parents. They will, of necessity, be intertwined. They will cover the same time. The approach will be different. Before we outline the programs as such, I will make a few observations about the commitments to be made by the different participants in the programs. We will discuss the age at which the Sacrament ought to be given to candidates and the reasons for these decisions. The different texts to be used by the candidates, their parents and sponsors merit some discussion. Service to the Church and to the community is part of the training program of the candidates. We will look at this item and note briefly the question of religious vocations. Finally, we will make note of the personnel involved in the program itself. Some, naturally, have specific roles to play. Others provide auxiliary services that complete the plan. When one of the members of the family is confirmed, this celebration can and must provide a very special occasion for a renewal of total commitment by everyone in the family, to God and to His Church.

The time during which the candidate is preparing for the reception of the Sacrament is a period of study and review of the commitment to be celebrated at the ceremony. The Liturgy of Confirmation does not make the commitment. It celebrates one already established. The commitment is considered from the viewpoint of several different people — the parents, sponsors, grandparents and other children in the family.

In the case of parents who have realized for years that they are the Church and who, with relaxed comfort, have been making basic decisions regarding themselves and their offspring, the commitment is secure. They have experienced the enormous psychological, spiritual and even physical benefits which accrue from that total commitment made many years prior to this time. Now, when they see their first or second or third offspring confirmed by their bishop they experience a very special feeling of euphoria. Their renewal is the cause of much happiness.

If the parents have not made a commitment of their lives to God, the present training program becomes their moment of truth and they must decide what to do about their situation.

Consider the grandparents who have watched with complete satisfaction the closeness of their own children to the Church. When they see their grandchild confirmed and observe the way in which the Church has cautiously combined the new and the old, they are practically amazed. They have had and will continue to have a strong spiritual relationship with the candidate. This only helps the candidate more to grow with the family in commitment. A well-established relationship like this, guarantees so much added force to the grandparents' and the parents' own commitment that it must be strongly encouraged and observed, lest anything rupture or injure it.

The children, whether it be the candidate or the other children, already have an awareness of their parents' total commitment to God and the Church. They have experienced with vivacity and intrigue how involved their family is with and in the Church. Their sophistication as members of the Church, in whatever capacity, is note-worthy. So at the ceremony of Confirmation and especially during the training program, all of them will themselves renew their own private commitments to God and to the Church and thus enable themselves to cope in some degree with all their future problems with reference to commitments. This, coupled to their parents' attitude, will bring added strength to the bond of family and the Church.

A final note can be made with regard to the commitment by the sponsors of the candidate for Confirmation. They, by the very essence of the role they play in the Confirmation program, must be part and parcel of the Church. In fact, the commitment they live by is the precise reason for their selection as sponsor for the candidate. They cannot function in the role without commitment. Their role enhances the commitment they profess.

• The Age for Confirmation

During the course of years, in the development of the pragmatics of the Sacrament of Confirmation, no question has been more elusive than that of the age of the candidate for the Sacrament. Many extraneous factors have controlled its determination. In some ages the Church has avoided the question by conferring Confirmation with Baptism. At other times in history the schedule of the bishop acted as the controlling force. Sometimes Confirmation took on the role of ancient puberty rites and was conferred on youngsters at any age between ten and fifteen. In days gone by, many parents and their children looked upon Confirmation as the terminal point in structured religious education. None of the above reasons or mentalities are in any way adequate to cope with the modern needs of our young people. The Sacrament of Confirmation is the liturgical recognition of the fact that the candidates are young adults in every sense of the word. They must be allowed to develop and mature, emotionally, spiritually, politically and sexually, before they assume the office of a confirmand.

This development will vary according to the individual but I think we can safely say that between the ages of sixteen and eighteen is the best time for most people to be confirmed.

It may take some communities several years to escalate their thinking and planning so that this age can be recognized as the ideal time for Confirmation. In our program, this situation is taken into account. Often it takes years for our people to understand and adjust to the ideal to which the now Church is leading us.

There is a final note to be made in regard to the ideal age for the reception of Confirmation. While most people readily acknowledge the age of sixteen to be much more realistic than any lower age, some are leaning toward eighteen as the ideal age for the reception of the Sacrament of Confirmation. They point out that the Congress of the United States, after a great deal of discussion and deliberation on the maturity of our young people, established by the 26th Amendment to the Constitution, the age of majority at eighteen. They note that this political move should tell the Church something of the times in which we live. We ought to capitalize on the situation by adopting this age of eighteen as the most proper time for young adults to receive liturgically the recognition of the Church of the legal fact of their adulthood. The idea has some merit. However, given the parental involvement with our candidates in the program to be outlined, the sixteen to eighteen ages might be the most practical and receptive ones.

In the preparation of a program for the candidates for the Sacrament of Confirmation, the textbooks to be used by the candidates and their sponsors and parents should be reviewed by the priest, religious coordinator and the committee.

The choice of books to be used in our program is quite serious and demands the attention of all. We must bear in mind the theme of our program: Adult Commitment. The texts we use must immediately convey to the candidate and his family this tone and theme. There is no shortage of texts from which to choose; some more attractive than others. Some are simply juvenile. They were meant to be used for youngsters making Confirmation. They could not possibly fill the need the candidates have for a mature presentation of the Sacrament. Others are based solely on modern psychology. They have very little theological, scriptural or liturgical depth. All these psychological insights are good but cannot serve as a basic text. Some decision must be made, however. I shall simply suggest two that to my mind fill the bill admirably.

Naturally, we presume that *The Holy Bible* and a copy of *The Decrees of the Second Vatican Council* will be basic. The text: *Confirmation: Official Rite and Commentary,* published by the Liturgical Press of Collegeville, Minnesota, seems to me to be the best for use by the candidate. It has ample background information and commentary to satisfy the needs of all. The inclusion, by way of introduction, of the "Apostolic Constitution on the Sacrament of Confirmation" by the Holy Father, establishes a tone in any program that is strong, efficient, up to date and, in truth, apostolic. The stress of the Constitution on "Community" and "Shared Priesthood" do much to put forth the mind of the Church in the administration of this Sacrament. A casual review of this text will show what a convenient liturgical and intellectual aid (and it is simply an aid) this can be in any planned program.

Another little pamphlet that can be of value to parents and sponsors is *Confirmation, Declaration of a Christian,* published by XXIII Publications of West Mystic, Connecticut. It has a schema that will give the parents a brief but adequate running commentary on the general outline that any program will certainly take. In a sense, it supplements very nicely the studies of their candidate and encourages them in their dialogue with their son or daughter. In this text, as a conclusion, we find two practical programs outlined that some may decide to follow, directly or indirectly, completely or in part.

A word might be said here about other aids to be used in the program. Again, there are many — some good, some bad. Our program must be looked upon as a living experience for the candidate rather than as a learning phase of life. The two, of course, cannot be divorced and any instrument that is beneficial to our total aim can be used as an aid. The danger is always that these aids can be and often are a hindrance to total effort by one or more of the candidates and/or by their instructors and tutors. Nothing will substitute for the personalism demanded at this time. A movie or filmstrip or drama can split the necessary connections better than anything else and we can waste a lot of time at no small expense to the community, with the use of these well-intentioned devices.

- **Service**

The program we will discuss for the preparation of candidates for Confirmation has a very specific and practical dimension that demands our preliminary attention. The candidates must be introduced to and given the occasion to exercise service in the Christian community. For some few candidates, this exercise will be a normal consequence of their decision to be a candidate for Confirmation. For others, it will be something of a surprise that it is part and parcel of their total training program.

Our program, with a built-in, structured requirement of a specific amount and type of service, precludes the possibility of critical and destructive attitudes on the part of everyone. It will be especially helpful to the young community and its members who might be embarrassed or reluctant to engage in such apostolic works. It has been our experience that we have not challenged the generous spirit of our young community to any great degree. We have not been hesitant to single out individuals for some specific work but, as a group, they have not been enlisted for any en masse dedication to a "youth in service" program. Our excuses have been many: the young people are too young to shoulder any serious responsibility; they are too busy with school or social affairs; they are mercenary. These excuses may have some foundation in fact, but the community cannot wait for these circumstances to change. We need their service now. We must give them the opportunity now to exercise a generous spirit of sacrifice in helping others.

During the past few years, we have experienced in the Church a dramatic decline in the number of young people who have shown a willingness to join the ministry or the convent. There are many factors involved in this situation, but I daresay that one of them is the fact that the young people have not been vigorously invited to join us in the service of the Lord. In a real sense, they have not had as a group an internship in service as they were maturing. As a consequence, many never even considered the possibility of dedicating their lives to God and the Church. We experienced a remarkable phenomenon some time ago. We watched many young people enlist in governmentally sponsored programs such as the Peace Corps and VISTA. This was done with little or no help from their Church. Despite this, some volunteered to do God's work both at home and abroad and they did so with great spirit and zeal. We should look on this fact as a sign of the times and capitalize on this experience.

Another aspect of this concept of service should be studied as a part of our program. As the candidates for Confirmation advance in spiritual and emotional maturity, they will be studying life in its many aspects. Their observations of life, married life, with all its vagaries and uncertainties in modern society will demand that they be well prepared for it long before they decide to accept marriage as their life's work. They may well conclude that they need a period in their lives dedicated to the principle of self-sacrifice. They may well decide to spend this time period, prior to their decision to marry, in a structured program of service to God and their community.

Our primary task during the time of their preparation for Confirmation is to equip them with precise attitudes that will enable them to make accurate decisions in the future. They will be trained as sophisticated agents in service to God and the community. The only way they can learn the mentality is by doing. Very often this is the secret device that opens the door to them and lets them into this new way of mature Christian living. The young people, once they are given the directive and the proper motivation for the project, are ingenious in finding ways to fulfill their service requirements.

This is an excellent occasion to introduce them to the concept of tithing with regard to their own time. The community can well use ten percent of their time. The work that they can do in their churches is almost endless, starting with the very lowly and extending to the loftiest. Every church can employ (without pay, of course) many young people in the simple cleaning and beautification of God's house and property. Every church can benefit from the young peoples' acceptance of the office of usher or the liturgical offices of lector or cantor at Divine Services. The opportunities in any community, outside the Church are just as diverse and multiple as in the Church. A casual look at the call for volunteers from hospitals, social service agencies, and political organizations provides the candidate with more than an abundant chance to fulfill his or her role as the adult Christian "in service." Again, his or her own choice will be a sign of maturity and zeal in "commitment."

The candidate's home and neighborhood are often fruitful fields for a person interested in being "of service." There is no need to go into detail. Time and again, we priests and ministers are weary trying to find someone to help an elderly and/or sick person in time of need. These candidates could almost establish an agency of their own to help people in their community. Periodically, we all need reminders that we can be "good Samaritans" and during this time of preparation for Confirmation, the candidates can be that "par excellence" and naturally enhance their own spiritual lives during their preparation period for their Sacrament.

We are not in the process of training our candidates

to be "do gooders." The young people of our day are much too worldly wise to be caught in that trap. With their street awareness, and perhaps because of it, they can clearly distinguish between fraudulent or contrived generosity and a real honest gesture of Christian service. We ought to encourage them to develop and use this enviable quality in their program for Confirmation. It takes more than mere encouragement. We must literally outline for them the specific rationale of the service requirements, the extent to which they must be involved and the precise motivation that this part of their training demands. Finally, they must interpret this requirement as a practical device to introduce them to their long-range plans for a dedicated adult life of service as members of the Christian community.

• Personnel

The preparation of a group of young adults for the reception of the Sacrament of Confirmation in the modern Church will, of necessity, involve a goodly number of people. Once we endorse as essential for this Sacrament, such an intensive, structured training program for the candidates, we commit ourselves to an involved exercise in community action. We would do well to catalogue the participants in the program and note the roles that the different people assume. It will clarify this collegial enterprise and help to assign the shared responsibility that will be involved in the whole program. A table of organization demonstrates the supportive emphasis that each member contributes to the entire plan: bishop and candidate; priest and tutors; parents and sponsors, and the community at large.

The candidate for the Sacrament is obviously the most important person in our whole program. Given the fact that the candidate is already mature, and quite well advanced in emotionalism, sexuality and spirituality, this person assumes, with the bishop, the twofold, primary responsibility of asking and giving Confirmation. This responsibility of the candidate involves the first large decision he or she may have to make. Many other decisions could hinge upon it. In fact, the candidate may well, at this time, be getting ready to marry or join the religious life. Encouragement and trust must be illustrated by all parties at this particular time. The status of the candidates will be enhanced a great deal by the close relationships that must prevail all during the training program.

• **Role of the Bishop**

If the concept of personalism so loudly proclaimed by the Fathers of the Council is to be a reality in our Church, the Sacrament of Confirmation provides a most practical and vivid opportunity for the bishop to demonstrate the principle. So seldom do our people have the chance to see their bishop, much less talk to him, that, at Confirmation, it becomes imperative that he not only be the minister of the Sacrament, the one presiding over the ceremony but that he also give these candidates, their parents and their sponsors some private time. With all due respect to the many serious calls on the bishop's time, none is more pressing than this opportunity. I am certain that to some, this urgency will seem not at all critical. The reason is that they have not experienced the results of this encounter in any parish — the awe and respect of the young candidate, the love, the gratitude of parents, grandparents, sponsors, etc., the admiration of observers and critics. All of these are of great value to our Church at this time.

The role of the bishop will be most significant, of course, at the conferring of the Sacrament but we cannot discount his very significant involvement in the actual program in any given parish or community. Naturally, he must be advised and be aware of any and all types of programs being administered in the diocese but he can greatly encourage the candidates and their parents by word, letter or policy either before, or certainly immediately after, the program starts. This gesture of a personal note to all the people involved in the program will do much to encourage them at this time when those at the parish level think of Confirmation as the most important thing that will happen in the parish during the year. Any gesture he can devise, given time and logistics, will be of tremendous help to everybody.

• Role of the Priest

When it comes to the program of preparing the candidates and their families for Confirmation, the priest is the primary agent. As such, he must work harder than anyone else on the project for two very specific reasons. First: his efforts provide the living example of the Church's personal concern for the candidate. Second, the rest of the people, the nuns, tutors, instructors, everybody will catch this spirit of dedication and will apply themselves diligently to guarantee the desired success of this program. He, the priest, will be the chief officer in the planning and directing of the program for a very special and rather simple reason — nobody else can do it, nor should they. It is remotely possible that a religious coordinator or a nun might have the competency in this area but they still do not have the "charisma" nor the responsibility to do this. They cannot come close to demonstrating the priestly concern needed here. It is of great importance for the priest to interview the candidate and his parents at the beginning of the program or even before it starts. Objections can be answered, doubts can be resolved, fears can be allayed and other allied problems can be done away with. This personal contact and concern will make the whole program another specific occasion for a renewal of total commitment by each family.

Furthermore, the priest himself must be the coordinator of all the roles in this endeavor. It is he who must guarantee that the relationship between parents and candidate is secure. It is he who must demonstrate the confidence that the Church has in our young people today. It is he who must show the candidate the theme of personalism and make certain that everybody else in the parish does the same. This is the opportunity for him to teach and to demonstrate to all the themes of personalism and collegiality. Finally, he must serve as liaison officer between his parish and the bishop.

• **Role of the Tutor**

The role of the tutor is probably the most delicate, and the most attractive one in the program. Whether tutors are religious or secular, men or women, they are the people closest to the candidate. It is they, in fact, who must convey to the young people the real message of the now Church in regard to Confirmation. They can detect the spirit of the candidate. They can direct and/or guide the person in time of decision or difficulty. For these reasons, they themselves must not only be very knowledgeable about all the teachings of the Church and about the opinions of various respected theologians but they must also be cognizant of all the inherent problems of our young people and thus capable of dealing with our youth in the now Church.

Another facet of the position of tutor is the fact that it provides the candidate with a closeness to a religious person who is not necessarily a Sister or Brother. The tutor is someone, outside their immediate family, who can provide an intimacy that will reveal the charm of the spiritual life in our times. Often, that is all that is missing in the candidate's search for direction in his or her future life in the Church. No one can minimize the importance of "personal touch" in fostering vocations to the religious life nor can one gainsay the beneficial memories that will help later on, whether in marriage or the religious life.

• **Role of the Parent**

The parents of a candidate for Confirmation have a unique and attractive role to play in the preparation of their son or daughter for this Sacrament. Their role has several dimensions and each one requires a bit of study for complete effectiveness.

In the preparation program, they are students in the now Church with the candidate. They will learn many new things about themselves and the Church during the training program. They will also be teachers of each other and the candidates in the process of their sons' and daughters' preparation. They will, in fact, all during the program, be in the process of demonstrating many of the principles of the program every day at home — authority, respect, etc.

Finally, the community will be given a lesson in youth relationships. This will not be an easy lesson to learn or teach. It will require prayer, discussion and decision.

The parents of the candidate must recognize the maturity of the decision "to be confirmed" that the candidate must make. They will support it by ratification. This whole process demands a delicate appreciation of their role in the training program.

• Role of the Sponsor

The first requirement of a sponsor is an awareness of the new mentality of the Church in regard to his office. This office is not a social token of a family relationship. Being invited to be a sponsor at Confirmation involves a sacred dedication to be with and to assist the candidate at any time in his future adult spiritual life in whatever way this is possible or demanded. Of necessity, this requires that the sponsor be entirely committed to God and to the Church. If this is not the case then this personal commitment must be effected before the ceremony.

To function effectively, the candidate's selected sponsor may well have to avail himself of the same program as the candidate. It may be that the teaching of the Church has come and gone without his knowing it. Certainly the texts used by the candidate in his training program can supply the demand.

• Role of Certain People in the Parish

It is a blessing that in the Church we have a few special people who can come to our assistance in almost any capacity. So it is with the program for Confirmation. There are over and above the aforementioned people who have very specific tasks. Always standing with the director, always ready to assist in many ways, are these members of the laity of the parish or community. It would be absurd to think of expediting any intensive program without their expertise and help. They must always be prepared to step in to the breach. They will be called upon to be substitute tutors. They will always be proctors, whenever and wherever they are needed. They may even have to step into the shoes of the priest-director on occasion. They will certainly be instructors in the liturgy, in the parts they know best as lectors, as acolytes and as sacristans. They are experts as ushers and collectors at Mass on Sunday. All these very important ministries must be maintained. They will do well to transmit to the candidates their quiet and unobtrusive apostolic spirit of service. They are experts in this regard and the candidates will benefit by association with them.

- ## Role of People of the Parish or Community

The people of the parish — last on the list of roles — are very important and most influential in the candidate's preparation for the Sacrament of Confirmation. They must encourage by their example. They must pray for and bless the candidates as often as they can. They must smile on them when they see them doing a good job. All the above will help immeasurably to advance the status of the candidates and to guarantee the feeling in the community of complementarity.

- ## Advertising the Program

A final preliminary note must be made before we discuss our program as such. We are all aware of the perpetually deaf ear given to pulpit announcements about many parochial affairs. When we commit ourselves to this program for Confirmation, we must be certain that everybody in the community hears about it. This necessity stems from the fact that the program involves many individuals not directly connected to the actual program. All the people should be aware of the influence they have on the success of the program and on the families of the candidates. In a real sense, we are looking for a community endorsement of the program. At the same time, we want to offer everybody at the time of Confirmation another "teachable moment" in their own spiritual lives. This can and must be done by a real public relations officer and not simply by a pulpit announcement.

The people have to be made aware of the new approach to Confirmation that the Church has inaugurated. They must be told that Confirmation is for adults. They must be acquainted with the advanced and mature subject matter in the program. They will be able to appreciate all the work and study required of the candidates once they understand the mentality of the Fathers of the Council who prepared for the now Church.

All that we tell the people at large about the program, in as many ways as we can — via pulpit, newspaper, radio, and television — will create a tone and atmosphere that will generate the necessary enthusiasm we need in the community. We must make them knowledgeable so that they can perform as a conscious, concerned community. Each member, in fact, becomes an agent in the plan to guarantee complete coverage.

A special effort may have to be made in regard to the young community. The program in its totality must become part of their vital happenings. It must be presented to them as a most sophisticated approach to their adulthood. It can have none of the trappings of juvenile group activity. The young people have to be shown that this program, their special, first adult encounter with God and the Church, is the "in thing" in modern Christian living. Even if it takes skyrockets and steel drums, it must be done.

Fortunately, our young people are smart. They learn fast. If the whole community is up on what the program is, and what it will do for the community then we will have no difficulty with our modern youth. In fact they will run way ahead of us.

● **Parents' Program**

A number of preliminary notations are in order before we discuss the actual program for the parents of the candidates for Confirmation. It is essential that the parents know that the program for them is a parallel study of the adult Christian in the modern world in conjunction with their candidate's study. It will be a structured dialogue on the Christian life according to the Second Vatican Council. They must become acquainted with the need in the Church today for knowledgeable and articulate parents. Once they understand the tone of collegiality in the program and the material for discussion in each session, they will be real partners with the priest and his team in the preparation of the candidates. With that stated we can go on to the actual program.

We have already said with regard to this Sacrament, that the primary concern is the candidate's decision: whether or not he is willing and ready to accept this development in his Christian commitment. Yet, this celebration of the Sacrament of Confirmation is to parents and godparents and/or the sponsor that the candidate chooses, a vital part in the spiritual growth of all concerned. So it seems to be that it is extremely important that we capitalize on this reality. When we address our attention to the parents, godparents and sponsors, we can see that this is an exciting time for them. Just short of the marriage of their child, his ordination to the priesthood or consecration in the religious life, this time in their family history is very, very serious. That is why the bishop is coming — to be with them at this time. This is a time for the Church family to work completely together on this project.

When we outline our program for parents and godparents, there will be, of course, a dozen objections to it. There is no need to mention these objections here. None of them, for all practical purposes, have any validity. In our "program for parents" I will use that term, "parents." The term includes godparents and sponsors. All these people should be instructed in or advised of the history of their roles in the Church community. For centuries, everybody understood that it was the responsibility of parents to take care of the religious nurturing and education of their offspring. It was not the job of the priests. It was not the job of the bishop. The job of the priest and bishop was simply to be at their beck and call at the key moment when the advancement in the child's spiritual growth was at a point that the services and the office of the priest and the bishop were essential. During the course of this last century, especially in our own country, the appreciation and execution of these roles were distorted. This came about for many reasons. We need not go into the mentality that was rampant when a Catholic school was built. The thought was: "Now the good Sisters or the good Brothers can take care of my son or daughter. I can relax." This, of course, was absolutely contrary to the mind of the Church, contrary to the normal responsibility, the primary responsibility of the parent to take care of the child's spiritual life. Happily, the Fathers of the Second Vatican Council put an end to this sort of thinking. Loudly and clearly they enunciated the principle of subsidiarity; that the larger organization would not step into the smaller one and, as it were, take all responsibility from it. Nor, as it was said by the Fathers, may the lower organization give to the higher organization its responsibility. The Fathers of the Council lost no time in saying loudly that there was a combination of responsibility here and that to guarantee this combination of responsibility between home and Church, between parent and priest there must be sessions of dialogue and discussion. This combination cannot be effected simply by a note sent from the priest to the parent or by an announcement from the pulpit.

In our modern Church, as well-intentioned, as well educated and as sophisticated as many of our people are, there are still a great many of them who have no idea what the Fathers of the Second Vatican Council really said. They have read the sometimes garish and flashy reports the daily press chose to publish but as far as having the feel of the Church and a knowledge of what the Fathers actually said, some of them are pathetically ignorant. This excuse has been given, "I have no time to read the decrees of the Council. You tell me what the Fathers said." Well, this is the time when we are going to be able to tell the people what the Fathers said. They have to be advised with regard to the primary doctrine, the primary decree of the Council, "the Church." They have to know what the Fathers said about the "Church in the Modern World." They must be advised about the thinking of the Church on marriage and the priesthood in the modern world. They must be aware of their own ministry and the ministry of their priests. The parents are interested. They want to know and they will take the time to come and dialogue about these decrees. They will respond. But they must know what is going to happen. There can be no evasion about what this program is. Once they are advised, once they know, their response will be vitalized by an interest and concern about their own spiritual lives and the lives of their offspring.

A great deal of this information can be given to these parents through the advertising program brochure long before they come to their first meeting of the program. The information they receive at this first meeting will be more specific and more detailed and should be introduced by a discussion of the pragmatics of the plan.

The first item of business, quite naturally, is to inform them of the number of sessions and the reasons we need that many. I have found that there are generally four sessions. Two of these sessions are conducted alone with the priest-director and the tutors of the candidates. Two of the sessions are conducted with the candidates present. Everyone is there: priest-director, tutors, parents and candidates. The reason for this is that there must be established, right from the beginning, once the people know the plan, a tone of solidarity and comfort. Everybody knows the entire plan. The second item of business, and this from a most practical point of view, is to inform all of the specific dates for the sessions so that we do not have conflicts with other important functions that will be going on in the community. All this as a start gives a very good tone to our collegiality.

Having established the tone of the plan, one must proceed immediately to outline the plan for everybody who is going to be involved. This must take the mentality of an overview. We start by saying: In the first half of our training program with your young people we will treat the Christian person in the modern world. It is a flashback, to the individual, practical progress that has been made up to this point with the candidate. It is a review of the family history, starting with the marriage of the parents and proceeding through the child's Baptism and First Communion, and covers his or her growth and development with its difficulties. This is the time to mention the more important decrees of the Second Vatican Council. I mention here simply: the *Decree on the Church in the Modern World;* the *Decree on the Liturgy;* the *Decree on Sacred Scripture.* We then proceed to convey to the people at this very first session the "tone" of the decrees. Here is where we strike at the very heart of the program we are now starting. We must mention: personalism, subsidiarity and collegiality. At the very beginning, as I mentioned above, it is well to clear away any problems so that there is no misunderstanding of the theme or purpose of the program.

The second session with the parents, "and this time it occurs with the candidates," takes place about a month after the first session. During that month they have had time to reflect, they have had time to pray, and they have had time to talk with the priest and with the tutors of the candidates. They have had time to talk with their own candidate. During the month they have had time to dwell on the items that have been discussed at the first session. Not only that, but they have had time to discuss with candidates all the things that have been discussed during the four sessions that the candidates have had with their priest-director and their tutors. This month is a most important period of time. It is a critical moment for the parent-candidate relationship. It demands a reaching out by the parents to the candidate in their parallel studies. It invokes a response from the candidate in return. During the month they have had time to just about decide whether they were going to go along with this system or not. They have had time to decide what they were really going to do in the next few months.

A notation must be made here with regard to the fact that it is exceptionally beneficial if both parents are able to attend these sessions. The temptation, of course, is always present for only one parent to come and then report back to the other. A big danger in this is the avoidance of the two-fold role of father and mother that has to be assumed in this project. Naturally, living in modern society, the call of other pertinent necessities of life may make it necessary for only one person to be able to be present at these sessions.

The subject matter of this conference is Baptism and Holy Eucharist. Both Sacraments are treated as focal points of the family's spiritual history. Both Sacraments, in the family and in the Church, illustrate the concepts of individuality and community. In the treatment of Baptism the discussion centers around the dedication and commitment that was made by the parents for themselves and the promises and investments they made for their child. The treatment of the Eucharist involves us in a discussion of the modern Christian at Mass and his developing appreciation and the difficulties and objections that modern people have with the Sacrifice of the Mass according to the new liturgy. Immediately, the *Decree on the Liturgy* of the Second Vatican Council comes into play. This is the time when an explanation of the decree itself must be made for the parents of the candidate and for the candidates themselves. Now is the time to put them to the test, as it were, and demand that a study of the decree itself be made at the leisure of both parents and candidate. Finally, there must be a short discussion of the practicalities of the law of the Church with regard to the Baptism of a child. The law of love of God, the law of love of reason must be discussed with both parents and candidate for an understanding of the interest that the Church has and the infinitely practical aspects of the new laws of the Church — the law of commitment, the law of community.

After another two months of time to meditate and study and pray over all the items that have been discussed, and are being discussed with the candidate, the parents come together once more with the priest-director and with the tutor to initiate, as it were, a turn and to further survey what is going to happen during the next several sessions with their candidate. There will be more food for thought, more food for meditation, more food for prayer. The theme to be announced immediately is that the next half of the training program will be entitled the "Mature Christian Person: Ripe for the Grace of Confirmation." Again a schedule must be given to the parents with the outline. It will include the following topics: Dignity and respect for their plans, and procedures that they will be making during the next several months with regard to the practicalities of their own preparation for Confirmation. Following the dignity and respect that the candidates deserve as gentlemen and gentlewomen, the topics will be responsible sexuality and obedience. The part given to the parents will be the quote from St. Paul. "Parents do not nag." Following close upon that will be a lengthy discussion of freedom and authority. Once again with the outline of the plan in hand and the overview clearly in their minds, the parents will relax all the more. They must be encouraged, lest perhaps fatigue or ennui discourage them.

Now is the time for priest-directors and their tutors

to give a progress report on the candidates. This should be done in a general way. This will give the parents some rule of thumb, as it were, a comparative study to help them in helping their candidate to make his decision, the decision to go forward with plans to accept the nomination as a candidate for Confirmation or the decision to delay because of some extraordinary or extraneous happening. They may decide that they don't feel they are ready to accept this Sacrament now. They may make the decision to wait for another time. In either case, they simply are not capable of accepting the Sacrament of Confirmation right now.

Now is the time for all problems to be discussed on a personal, individual basis. There may be some reluctance to bring any of these problems to the attention of the priest-director. Hence, he must demand that the parents and tutors use good sense and do what they know is right. Then he himself, the priest-director, will have to cope with the problem with great expertise because some of these problems will demand it. Of course they must be handled with the kindness of Christ Himself, knowing full well how difficult the situation is for the parents and the candidate.

Finally, at this session, the most sensitive and most important subject of vocations to the adult life must be discussed, with emphasis on the possibility of a call to the religious life. Now is the time to be certain, with great delicacy, that there is no obstacle put in the way of a candidate by his or her parents. It may seem difficult for us to envision that at this late date in Church history this is still going on, but there are parents who themselves have almost an angry fear that their child may be called to the priesthood or to the religious life. Their reasons are varied and strange, but very real to them.

We must guarantee the Church that we will cope with the problem now. We need parents with a good mental outlook. They must encourage by attitude and word their young people so that they can accept this calling to the religious life. Parents must make it appear attractive to the young people in this modern age. A little cautious prodding could well keep any grace of a religious vocation in good condition.

The fourth and final session with the parents is almost a prayer meeting rather than a lecture. The parents at this session, with their candidates sitting beside them, exhibit a thankful pride and satisfaction. They know and feel the accomplishment that has been going on over the past months. They are experiencing a holy excitement as they see their project coming to its climax. The subject matter itself is rather like a series of links in a chain, all necessary components in the life of the candidate, all of them dependent on one another to make the strength of the candidate that will be obvious at the time of his or her Confirmation. The first topic under consideration is Christian Joy, a well-founded virtue stemming from the obvious spiritual growth and maturity of the candidate and the joy of unity with his parents and his Church. The parents themselves take a great deal of joy in watching their sons and daughters in their own growth and maturity. This joy leads to the basic virtue of love, a mature self-appreciation by the candidates, a humble appreciation of everybody else. This has to be mentioned to the parents of the candidate so that they can themselves take more joy in what they see. Another serious topic: The freedom of the candidates, a freedom for something, comes next. It is especially important for parents to realize at this time freedom in their candidates' lives. This freedom for development must be fostered with loving care. The young people are in search of a way of life, they must be nourished in this freedom for life with God in religion or with another person in love. The entire collage provides the parents with fruitful material for self-examination. It gives them both encouragement and caution lest they love too much or love too little, lest they demand too much or demand too little. The final item, the twofold authority and obedience nuance, brings them back to cold reality. Examples from Sacred Scripture, hagiography, casual observation of modern society and education will not guarantee the perfect exercise of both of these necessary qualities of life, but prayerful study and dialogue with their candidate will do much to reach the ideal for which we all hope and pray.

We will mention a few more items of interest to parents after we have discussed the program for the candidates. I include here some outlines for the several sessions of dialogue between the parents, priest and tutors. They contain all the items that need treatment. They can be narrowed or broadened as the individual case warrants.

- **Parents' Program Outlines**
Session 1
    A. Purpose of Parents' Program
        Content and general outline
    B. Purpose of Candidate's Program
        Content and general outline
    C. Emphasis: Scriptural
                  Liturgical
                  Practical
    D. Roles in Program
        History
        Distinction: Home—Church

Parent—Priest—Bishop
Vatican II
E. Adulthood of candidate
Decision: "To be confirmed"
F. Expectations: Candidate
Parents
Church

G. Calendar
H. Decrees of Vatican II
 I. Tone of decrees: Collegiality
Subsidiarity
Personalism

J. Pragmatics

Session II (Candidate Session 4)
Introduction: Togetherness in: Study
Dialogue
Development

A. Baptism:
1. Individuality of candidate
2. Parents' commitment
3. Community involvement
4. Guarantees to God and Church
5. Insurance of development
6. History of liturgy
7. Ritual—Vatican II

B. Holy Eucharist
1. Decree on Liturgy
2. Mentality of parents
3. Example and practice of parents
4. Problems and difficulties of candidates
5. Status of communicant in Church
6. Role of communicant in community

Session III
- A. Progress report
  By priest — tutor — parent
  Of candidate's: Study, Prayer, Activity
- B. Review: Schema: Christian person
- C. Preview: Plan: Dialogue
  Subjects: Maturity, etc.
  Competence: Candidate
- D. Pragmatics: Decision of candidate
  Attitude of sponsor
- E. Examination of candidate
  Private
  Public
- F. Problems
- G. Expectations
- H. Vocations

Session IV (Candidate Session 12)
- A. Review of purpose of program
- B. Review of progress of candidate
- C. Discussion:
  Joy — Freedom
  Love — Obedience
  Maturity — Authority
- D. Use and abuse practicalities:
  Money
  Cars
  Life
- E. Summation
- F. Examination
- G. Pragmatics
- H. Liturgy for Confirmation

• Candidates' Program

I would ask the reader to bear in mind while surveying the candidates' program all we have said about the parents' program, especially the combined purpose of each. Both parents and candidates must understand the correlation of their different programs and the total effect of each one.

These general effects and purposes can be presumed to be known by all from the advertising program, but they will be repeated and refined, again and again, during the course of the training period.

One should also assume that the candidates have become aware of some of the concepts in the program. The most important idea is that we are engaged in a very adult program — a sophisticated exercise in adult community living. The candidates must assume this certain posture to participate in the program.

A number of preliminary notes are essential here before we go into the details of the actual program. All candidates for Confirmation are adults. They are young, they are adolescent, but no one can be confirmed in this program unless they are adults. They are to be addressed as "men and women" and they are to proceed as gentlemen and ladies. At first some of the candidates will be almost embarrassed when they are addressed in this manner. This may well be the very first time that they have been addressed as "Mr. or Miss or Ms." Their very first function, as such, must be to make formal application for admittance to the program. This gesture immediately establishes them in a special category. They have never experienced this formality in the Church before in their lives. Prior to this, their parents took all responsibility. To enhance the formality, it would be wise to have applications printed that must be obtained from the parish secretary's office. These applications would contain, over and above all pertinent vital statistics, such as name, address, etc., a short, simple questionnaire, but one revealing to some extent the mentality of the candidate at this time. Before they even start their training program, we want to know how much they know now about the Church and what they expect of us in the Church. The questionnaire is a bit of a shock and puzzlement to them. Yet they also begin to suspect how deeply interested we are in each one of them, personally. A note to this effect should be printed on the questionnaire itself.

The application should also request a short statement from the candidate: "Why I want to be confirmed." Some will give the stock answers. Others will, after some thought and discussion with their parents, come up with some very interesting insights which in the long run, will help both them and us in their training. The application should carry a line for the signature of the parents of the candidate and perhaps even one for the candidate's godparents. This endorsement of the candidate's application creates, immediately, a sense of collegiality in the family from the very start of the program. To maintain this formality, a receipt of the candidate's application should be sent out to him or her. A small significant secretarial task such as this could well be the responsibility of the liturgy committee of the parish council. It will signify some formal community involvement.

Just before the first candidate session, the date should be announced formally. It should be a simple announcement: "We will start the Confirmation program in our parish (time, date, place) with 'X' number of young people who have shown by their statements their intention that they are serious young adults. We will pray for them every day until the bishop comes to confirm them." This formal announcement will generate in the person of the candidates a certain excitement, and in the people, a quiet, proud interest. Everybody wants to see young people grow in their spiritual lives and this Sacrament will mark them as young people well on their way in the life of the Church and of society.

Our next preliminary consideration is how long the formal program of preparation should last. We abstract from the very lengthy, remote preparation, of course, because it is presumed that the candidate has been under preparation for many years. At the very least, one full calendar year should be the norm. This can be extended to eighteen months in a case where the candidates or group of candidates, and/or their families are found to be unprepared for such an intense program. It may be necessary and even advisable to take eighteen months but the "one year" rule of thumb gives all involved adequate time, without any rushing or any anxiety but with prayerful comfort, to make adequate preparation for the holy reception of the Sacrament of Confirmation. This time interval gives the candidate an opportunity to study his initial decision to apply for admission to the training program. This is basic and the decision cannot be rushed. It must be renewed many times during the period. The candidate must be reminded again and again that he is in the process of making a "developing commitment" to God and the Church. This takes time. Secondly the parents and the godparents, even though their decision in regard to their child's Confirmation is secondary and only supportive of the candidates, also need time to study and pray over their own role in the conferring of this Sacrament. They need time to review and to renew their own commitment to God and the Church.

One of the most important parts of this Confirmation program is the dialogue that must occur between the parents of the candidates and the candidates themselves. It is possible that there could be obstacles, even at this late date in the lives of the candidates to sincere and open discussion of the subjects contained in the program with their parents. Presumably there will be none. All need plenty of time to absorb and discuss each topic in the program. No time will be lost, but they need all they can get. Finally, there must be time for dialogue between the parents and the tutors and critique of the candidates. Sometimes the very logistics of this necessary element demands a whole year so that the ideal of "personalism" can be effected. It would be painful after everything else is effected if this special part of the candidate's preparation for Confirmation were neglected. This personal and collegial meeting of the minds is especially significant to the candidate's understanding of his or her Church family.

The very first meeting with the candidates is one of "introduction." It is extremely important. First impressions, especially with our young people, will carry through. The tone of the session must be strictly formal. This is not a first day of fun and games. This is big business. The presence of the whole parish committee demonstrates this. All the priests of the parish, all the nuns and Brothers, everyone concerned. All the people working on this program will do well to present themselves at this first meeting. It helps to set the atmosphere. The candidates have to receive a formal, friendly welcome. This can be extended by one or by several of those present at the meeting: the pastor himself and/or the president of the parish council, someone with dignity, authority and official distinction. It need only be a simple, sincere statement of the great expectations the whole parish has for the success of the candidates in this new program; the trust, confidence, hope that we have in them; the prayers we will be saying for them. Finally, this strong statement must be made with force, clearness and sincerity. This statement: "Nobody has to be here; you are here because you decided to come. Nobody made you come. If you made a mistake in your decision to come, that is perfectly understandable. If you did, please leave now. We have a great deal of work to do here and we need 100 percent effort, so get it straight from the beginning" establishes the proper tone. Once this atmosphere is created the prayer of the Council Fathers can be said: "We are here before you O Holy Spirit, etc." This prayer is always proper but most especially at this first meeting. This same prayer might be used at every session but any other suitable prayer might be selected. As times goes on, a candidate could be assigned to compose a prayer himself and read it for the group.

Having secured the proper atmosphere, the director can proceed to the business at hand. To give some direction to their own minds and talents at this first meeting, the candidates can be given an outline of the plan for the first semester: an overview of half of the project — and half will be enough. With a copy of the outline in their hands they will be able to follow, as it were, the map as to where they are going. In one sense this schema will overwhelm them; in another, it will relax them. Much will seem familiar to them and they will wonder why we will be talking about Baptism or about the Mass. They will soon find out. We must immediately explain that they are not children, and that they cannot act and pray and live as children now. They are candidates for Confirmation. They must be equipped with modern Second Vatican Council knowledge and practices. They may even be given samples of the problems facing young people today, because they cannot cope with life and religion — the number of young people who do not go to Mass unless someone "makes" them, the way the Sacrament of Confession has been neglected or abandoned because people don't think they need it, the serious confusion that is rampant in young married people in our country and in our Church today. Many other items could be cited. We simply want to demonstrate the necessity for an investigation into these Sacraments if we are going to live as mature Christian persons in the post Vatican II Church. We ought not to be concerned if the candidates seem a bit skeptical at this time. As we dig into these matters they will begin to see how uninformed they are. They will in due time appreciate the whys and the wherefores of the whole plan.

To expedite their preparation for Confirmation, the candidates should have the use of several texts mentioned earlier in this chapter. A word of explanation is in order. Their Bible will be a prayer book as well as a reference book. The different decrees of the Council can well serve as a source of meditation. The liturgy books are studies of the Church in life and prayer. All the texts must be put to all the different uses that can be found for them.

This brings us to the most important item that will probably concern us and the one which will require our attention during the whole course. That item is the "attitude" that the candidates have. We know it is good now but they must be warned about the future problems that they will have to face. The first one is the pressure that will come from their peers who have no concept of what is happening. Sometimes a carping criticism of the candidates will be in evidence. Young people by nature can be cruel; yet they are very sensitive. These candidates must be strengthened and encouraged, lest this peer pressure gets to them and they abandon their goal. Adverse pressure can even come from members of their own family. This is worse. They have many projects to carry out at home and any ridicule will make things extremely difficult for them. Finally, there is the problem of fatigue from the very busy schedules that they maintain. This fatigue could be detrimental to their preparation for Confirmation. Merely mentioning these items, even with understanding, will not make them disappear, but at least the candidates will be forewarned and strengthened by our solicitude. We need to repeat our concern several times during the course of the semester.

Having heard all of this, they will be looking for some sort of an assignment to start them off. These are the things they should be told. Now that they have a copy of the general plan they must make a private plan of their own. This will include a new type of daily prayer in addition to, or in place of, their usual way of praying. They could use the passages of Sacred Scripture given in their text relating to Confirmation. They could use the Psalms, reading a different psalm, each day, but they have to start some private plan for prayer immediately. The same applies to study. They could plan to read part of the *Decree on Sacred Scripture* or part of any other decree but they should start immediately. They could select their patron saint from Baptism or a new patron for their Confirmation name and start to read a biography of that particular saint. They must start to select the service that they are going to perform during the course of their preparation. All we need demand now is that they get busy and outline their own private plan. A part of this is the notebook that they will be using. This notebook could serve as a log for them or they may choose to keep a separate log that could be an excellent memento of the whole year. It might serve well at future times to help renew their young vibrant spirit. Some may even choose to keep a diary. Finally, the candidates are advised that they and their parents will have an interview with the director or his delegate. This announcement will not be received with any great enthusiasm by the candidates but it is best that they have the information now so that they can talk about it among themselves and perhaps even with their parents. All in all they know what to expect and they will not be disappointed.

Once the candidates are clearly familiarized with the general plan, they can be guided, session by session, through several discussions which will help them to appreciate the meaning of the mature, modern Christian person, which is the theme of the whole semester. It must be demonstrated to them, in many ways, that this must be the fact. Before they are confirmed they must be, and know that they are, mature, modern, knowledgeable Christian persons. In brief this means a short study of some of the decrees of the Second Vatican Council and a review of the meaning of all the Sacraments with the application of each to the lives of the candidates.

The second session with the candidates will give them a broad view of the teaching of the Fathers of the Second Vatican Council. It will make them alert to the themes of the Council.

The third session with the candidates will give them an appreciation of the sacramental system with its scriptural and liturgical implications. More time than I have allotted to these studies can be given to them. This will depend on the circumstances of the individual parish.

The Second Vatican Council's first decree to be published was *The Constitution on the Sacred Liturgy* and, naturally, this decree will be preeminent in the discussions that will be carried on during this time. Close upon it will be *The Decree on Sacred Scripture*. These two decrees are the most practical ones for the candidates, and every discussion on every Sacrament must have the twofold flavor of Sacred Scripture and Liturgy.

We might mention here a caution — a fact in the preparation of the candidates. Many of these candidates have heard very little of the First Vatican Council or the Council of Trent. We must bear in mind that the parents of these candidates have grown up under the influence of the First Vatican Council and they know quite a bit of the theology and the practices of the pre-Vatican II Church. Many items of the First Vatican Council can and do fit in very well with this program. The candidates must be reminded of this, lest, in the dialogue with the parents, they fall into the error of thinking that all their parents know is old-fashioned and has been dismissed by the teaching of the Second Vatican Council.

It is proper right away in the second conference to give the candidates a rundown on all the decrees of the Council. Naturally it is impossible for them to read very many. As a matter of fact they may end up by reading only *The Decree on the Liturgy* but they should be familiar with the scope of all the decrees of the Council. If they are going to be "the Church" they should know what and who the Church is and how she is to function in the modern world. With a copy of the decrees in their hands, and at home, we can have some hope that they and their parents will dip into them or consult them on occasion. Possibly even more important to impress on the minds of the candidates is the thrust of all the decrees of the Council. I list three here: collegiality, subsidiarity and personalism.

It is impossible, within the limits we have, to do much more than mention these great ideals of the decrees but we must spend some time in illustrating the principles to the candidates. By this time they are already aware of them working in their own lives. A formal discussion of the principles will only make the candidates more secure in their present role in their family and in their Church. As time goes on they will feel how beneficial these themes of the Council are to them personally. As we proceed into the discussion of the Sacraments they will understand just how deeply the Fathers of the Council had them in mind all during their deliberations.

Once the candidates are imbued with the "spirit" of the decrees of the Council, then in the third session, it is a simple process to take them through the sacramental system, with special emphasis on the liturgical and scriptural aspects of all of them. It is well to give them the bird's-eye view — a total picture of the seven ways given by Christ for very special assignments, at different times and in different circumstances of life. Often the young people are wont to pigeonhole the individual Sacrament. It is well to give them the overview with the interlocking influences of each. This is especially true of the Sacrament of Confirmation and the Sacraments of Marriage and the Priesthood.

There is no better exemplification of the hidden theology in every Sacrament than that found in the actual administration of them. This is important for those being confirmed. They must understand the connection between the commitment made by their parents, at their Baptism, and the commitment they themselves will make at Confirmation. This is the time to illustrate to them the impact on the community of all the Sacraments. It is very difficult for young people to understand this concept of "community" but introducing them to it now, and repeating it with each individual Sacrament will help them immensely to understand the idea and get the feel of it. One of the more serious problems that we have today with our youth is the feeling of lonesomeness that they seem to be exhibiting constantly. This idea of community in conjunction with their spiritual lives in the sacramental system may help them. As we said before in the discussion on the Sacrament of Holy Eucharist, the idea that we are God's family will be very helpful in their mental and spiritual growth.

Some of the pragmatics of the Sacrament often open up to the candidate many of the ideas that we have already discussed — the encounter with God and the Church, the dependence and the involvement of the individual. These privileged moments, as it were, all in a very practical way, help the person to feel community status and satisfaction. This is probably the final note with which to conclude every session on the Sacraments. When they see the sacramental system is not just a lot of academic theology but the living Church family in everyday experience, with all its ramifications, they will then appreciate how vital it is that they themselves use every part of the system for their own personal growth as mature Christians.

The next three sessions, or if time permits, even six, can be given over to a detailed study of each of the Sacraments. Now that the revision of the liturgy for all the Sacraments has been completed, it will be somewhat easier to consider them and demonstrate them to the candidates. They themselves will show intense interest as they carry on their own programs and see how their lives in the Church, at the moment, and the things they do in preparation for Confirmation will be the foundations for their lives in the future, in marriage or in religion. By the end of the treatment of all the Sacraments they will have a total view of the well-developed Christian person and an appreciation of how close they are to becoming such.

A reference to the outlines at the end of this chapter will demonstrate that the last three sessions on the individual Sacraments are not a rehashing of a child's catechism. They give a new approach, a new direction, a new dimension to the candidate's understanding of the life of grace in liturgical action. They involve adult maturity, modernization and total commitment, the sum total of our combined efforts in this enterprise.

• Second Semester

It often happens, in many communities, that the calendar for this program for Confirmation parallels the school calendar and the end of the first part of the program coincides with the Christmas holidays. Even if it does not, there should be some interlude before the second section of the program is started. This is not absolutely essential but the hiatus gives some relaxed time for rest and review.

Once the candidates have completed the first part of their program, the chaff will have been separated and all of them will be ready to move on and move quickly. At the initial meeting of this part of the program, the director will do well to give them a renewed spirit and strength that they will need as they go forward. Right away a review is in order. It is not so much a review of the material covered in the first part of our program but more of a review of the mentality of "maturity" on the part of the candidates: how closely they have been in dialogue with their parents; how well they have maintained their own private schedules of study, prayers, and services, etc. A sharp critique is in order now and this critique must be made by the candidates with the help of their director, tutors and parents. This is the time to restate the basic principle, blunt as it is — "Nobody made you come here. If you have not produced, please leave." The spirit and tone of the program must be renewed and intensified. The candidates are expected to finalize their decisions to present themselves to the bishop to be confirmed and to do this their spirit must be sharpened.

In the first meeting of the second semester, the general outline of the plan will be given to them. This plan and outline will be possibly more exciting to the candidates than the material of the first semester. The subject matter of this semester is part of daily living for them. They will be concerned and perhaps even anxious about what the outcome will be. The subjects of freedom, authority, obedience, good manners, sexuality, are part of their day-by-day maturing process. At this session they ought to be given, if possible, the calendar, even to the point of the exact date of the actual administration of the Sacrament of Confirmation. Some date of the coming examination should be noted. Perhaps it would be better to call the examination a qualifying session. We are not in academics. We are in the business of Christian living. Some of the candidates would fail an examination in the ordinary sense of the word but assigning a date for a possible demonstration in church or at home of all they do know, will allow them to set their own timetable and start making practical plans.

It does the people of the parish good to observe them in this qualifying mentality. The candidates become tired of hearing "mature Christian persons," but they know when they are juveniles, when they exhibit childishness. The next few months of their training is very personal to each one of them. They are constantly on exhibition at home, in school, socially, by and in the church. They are being watched and judged by each other, by their parents, by other members of the family and the community. This should be helpful to them. All during this time, prior to Confirmation, they need encouragement and this must be given by all concerned.

The theme and the thrust of these sessions is to examine the qualities of the mature Christian person. This survey encompasses different aspects of the manifestations of the adult Christian, as well as some of the basic issues that have to be dealt with in our daily lives. The thrust of this part of our program is to be sure the candidates know these "basics" and are qualified to cope with any of the accompanying problems. All of them will be constantly asked, "Are you an adult?" If you are, then you must understand obedience, joy, authority and freedom. In order for them to understand all of the subjects, they must discuss each at some length.

Here again, the number of sessions can vary, and the subject matter can be covered singly or in groups of two or even three. These subjects are essential for Christian living and therefore we must spend as much time as is needed in studying each item. Another practical note is to set up a few good norms for the group of young people to carry out throughout their lives. Many times, youthful "competition" can destroy reasonable norms for good conduct. This can be avoided in this group by study, discussion and prayer to set up mature and Christian standards.

I will list the items here and comment only briefly on them. The outlines at the end of the chapter show in detail how they must be examined at length. The first is dignity. With all that we have discussed in the first session about the Christian person, this first item is a natural consequence. It is very difficult for young people to overcome their natural embarrassment when talking about themselves, and to understand the great dignity which they do have and must find in each other. Allied to their dignity is the normal respect they must have for themselves and for each other. Both of these find outlets in countless everyday circumstances. We adults try constantly to keep these qualities in mind with our social intercourse. Just in observing the normal amenities of life we expect to find good manners in everyone. In the minds of the candidates, however, this is not so easy. Very often a simple demonstration of all the above together will help them to understand and pursue them. There is no area in life in which the above factors should operate more forcefully or more importantly than in the development of the candidate for Confirmation.

We know, in this world today, there is no lack of sex knowledge, good, bad and indifferent, in our candidates. Since childhood they have been exposed to every sort of picture, joke and/or movie depicting sex. We know this has done nothing for their sexuality. They are just as much in need of assistance in their sexual development as any other generation. If we can start our discussion of sexuality, in all its phases, knowing that they already have an understanding of dignity, respect and good manners, the more intricate parts of the discussion of their sexuality will be that much easier for them to absorb and to understand. The success or failure of future marriages will be contingent upon how well they understand their own sexuality and are comfortable and secure in it. The session on sexuality need not be long and drawn out, but it must be thorough, realistic and not overly pious.

As we stated earlier, our candidates feel that they are now developed people. The next four subjects, taken together or separately, give added motivation for insight into themselves and each other. We presume that this insight gives them joy at what they see and that they can proceed to exercise this joy in discussing freedom, obedience and authority. It does not make a bit of difference how or in what order these topics are discussed. The candidates and their parents, the schools, and the Church, all know that these factors of life are pulsating every minute of the day everywhere. The balance between them is shifting all the time. When there is a dialogue between all parties, however, there is less likely to be misunderstandings or ruptures. How much freedom do they need? How much authority can they handle? How obedient are they? The examination can go on forever and it must for every individual person and situation. The more meditation and dialogue there is, the more understanding and concert there will be.

As difficult and involved as the items of this part of the training program are for the candidates and their parents, it is essential that they be there. The structured dialogue that is involved almost guarantees the ideal maturity demanded of the candidates and the collegial responsbility of their parents. The burden of parents is tremendous in these areas of spiritual development in their families. We can do no better than to help them shoulder it. The encouragement we give will be evident in the interviews and consultations that we have with the can-

110

didates and their parents during the training program, prior to the actual ceremony of Confirmation.

• **Conclusion**

After the candidates have completed their formal training program with their tutors and their priest-director, there is one more small exercise that can be effected. This informal session can be a fitting transferral of their interests from their intense mental and emotional preparation to a more cultic atmosphere.

It is remotely possible that even after all the discussion, and all the training, and all the work in and around the Church, the candidates still may not have the familiarity with the church building and the ecclesiastical accouterments that they should have. They have read in *The Decree on the Liturgy* the general norms for building and renovating churches to accommodate the people of God in their community worship. It would do the director well to give them a tour of the church, be it ever so humble. An intimate visual scan of the actual locale of the administration of all the Sacraments does something for these well-prepared candidates. It gives them a relaxed closeness to the Lord Himself. It makes them comfortable. This will help them psychologically in the ceremony of Confirmation. They will feel the strong personal bonds in God's House between God and the bishop, between God and themselves with the bishop. This is just another helpful item in their preparation.

At the conclusion of the training program, the director and tutors will have a few practical items with which to attend. These may seem trivial in view of all that has preceded. We know the candidates are well-prepared to receive the bishop and the Sacrament of Confirmation, but this is not time for laxity. The high standards so well-established at the beginning must be maintained now. The effect on the candidates and on the parish at large will serve to demonstrate the thoroughness of our interest and concern for them. Our young people are now hopefully operating on an effective adult level and they will expect as much.

There must be a review of each candidate, his service record must be certified by a responsible agent as to the fact of his service and the quality thereof. There should be an examination of each candidate either by the parents at home — and that is probably the best way to do it — or by the tutor or the director, either publicly or privately. The log or notebook of each candidate should be scanned as well as the report on the saint whose name will be chosen for Confirmation. We have not made as much of this as we might have. All the candidates might well give an oral report to their associates on the saint whom they have chosen. Hagiography at this stage of their development can give them a taste of the world and of Church history which can serve them well.

Another item that will really formalize their final round of preparation is a personally written note to the bishop. They should give their qualifications and reasons why they think they are ready now to be confirmed. They should also state, insofar as they can, their future plans as confirmed adult Christians. They might even give a projection of what kind of Catholics they will be in five years. What will be their goals; what kind of adult Christian education will they engage in; and what will be their basic practices; what part they will play in the apostolate? This note to the bishop may seem uncalled for to some. However, when you consider the seriousness with which these people will write these items down for the bishop, we might well have here, in writing, the commitment we are all seeking. They may be committed to God and the Church without the note but with it will go a formality that could well establish that commitment forever.

At some time before the ceremony of Confirmation, everybody — the priest, tutors, parents, sponsors and candidates will gather together. This may happen at a special meeting, at the rehearsal for the ceremony, or at a liturgy of the Eucharist before Confirmation, should the Sacrament be conferred outside Mass. At this time the pastor or director will take the opportunity to instruct the people to "celebrate" with their candidate in joyful thanksgiving. This is the immediate preparation for the coming of the Holy Spirit. A celebration is indeed in order and it will culminate with the conferring by the bishop of this great Sacrament.

Before we speak of the ritual of Confirmation itself we must say a word about a special Eucharistic celebration, in the event that the bishop does choose to confirm apart from Mass. This celebration, whether offered privately by the director and the candidates, or with the parents and sponsors present, can be and should be a really emotional experience for all present. All the readings, hymns, psalms of the liturgy are a brilliant overture to the celebration about to come in Confirmation. Everyone is so pleased with the candidates and they themselves are so pleased with each other, that a holy electricity can be detected. Variations for this liturgy are numerous and a committee should have no difficulty in making proper and particular selections to fit the occasion.

The variety of choice for the actual celebration of the Sacrament of Confirmation depends on the feelings of the bishop or pastor. Basically, the decision must be made whether to confirm within the Mass or outside it. It would be more than presumptuous to direct the hierarchy in our country in the liturgy of which they are most competent. Nonetheless, it seems to me that, in general, we have two situations. The first is where the number of candidates is small — under twenty-five. In this case the bishop could celebrate the Eucharist with the people and still have some time to dialogue directly with each individual candidate and his or her parents and sponsor. In the second case, where the group is larger, it would better serve our purposes if the pastor or director offered the Eucharistic celebration at some time just prior to Confirmation, and not on the day of Confirmation. The people will get the same results. Then the bishop can spend his time with the candidates when he simply confirms them. As another practical point, the priest can read the Sacred Scripture to them and lead them in a renewal of their baptismal vows in the separate ceremony. As a matter of fact, this should be done before they are allowed to approach the bishop, making the occasion as it were, a special prelude to their entering church. Then, when they approach the bishop, in very small groups, they will be keyed up, spiritually and emotionally, for the great happening. The bishop himself will appreciate this obvious spirit and reply in kind.

The total liturgy of the Sacrament of Confirmation, whether it be conferred within the setting of the Mass or not, is extremely important to our whole program. It is a very dramatic presentation of the modern Church in collegial activity. It is the Church in total dynamics; the whole family of God celebrating. The candidates and their families have put a great deal of effort into preparing for the enterprise. They are offering the bishop a guarantee of their families' commitment to the Church and he in the name of all God's people is graciously accepting it.

The ceremony is an emotional and spiritual experience for these parents. It is the climax of personalism for them. When the bishop speaks to them, when they see the reaction of their children as the bishop speaks to them, they will be grateful to God for all the energy and grace that they have received to help them function as they have in the program.

After the ceremony, in the next week or month, there should be a social meeting for all the candidates and their parents. This is not essential, of course, but from the point of view of the parish family this affair can aid considerably in introducing people, in allowing them to socialize. They have prayed together, they have studied together. They deserve on occasion to celebrate together socially. This simple celebration makes it much easier for them to function as a Church family in the more serious phases of Church life.

A final responsibility the parents of the candidates may accept is to write a critique of the program itself or any part of it. This critique will be for future planning by the priest and the committees of the parish. It will in no small way help the bishop himself and his staff in diocesan research and development. Some may be more reluctant to do this than others. Many will see the value in giving the critique and will feel competent to do so. They will see this as a real challenge in their Church.

Finally, the parents of the candidates must be exhorted to continue with their vitality in other areas of Christian living beyond the preparation of their child for the Sacrament of Confirmation. They will be able to do this with added force and enjoyment now that they have lived with their priest, their bishop, their son or daughter in the collegiality of the now Church family.

The candidates ought to be given by the parish some token of recognition as adult members of the Church. They have demonstrated their competence as adults and will be expected to perform as committed adult Christians in the Church. A small memento of the occasion of their Confirmation is also in order. It might be something as simple as a Rosary. They could keep it and use it until their own children are confirmed.

• Outlines of Subject Matter

The following outlines in this manual are to be used as a general guide to the priest-director of the Confirmation Program. They are strictly topical. Each one of the subjects could be the study of a lifetime. Each director may have to pick and choose according to his own circumstances. I have found them adequate in giving the candidates, their parents, and their sponsors, a picture of the well-informed committed Christian in the modern Church.

• Candidates' Program Outlines
Session I
    General Schema
      1. Teaching of the Church
          Vatican II
          Decrees: Liturgy
                    Religious Freedom
                    Laity, etc.
      2. Requirements
          A. Religious Practices

B. Use of Bible
C. Role of Candidate
D. Role of Parents
3. Equipment
    A. Bible
    B. Decrees of Council
    C. Texts on Confirmation
    D. Program Guide
    D. Log
4. Procedures
    Lecture
    Discussion
    Decision for Practical Action
5. Program Guide
    Modern Christian Person
    1. Decrees of Vatican II
    2. Themes of Vatican II
    3. Sacraments
    4. Baptism and Penance
    5. Eucharist and Confirmation
    6. Marriage and Priesthood

    Adult Christian Person
    1. Maturity
    2. Dignity — Respect
    3. Sexuality — Gentility
    4. Authority — Joy
    5. Freedom
    6. Obedience

Session II
    1. Decrees of Vatican Council II
        A. The Church: God's Community
    2. Tone of Decrees

117

      A. Personalism
      B. Collegiality
      C. Subsidiarity
  3. History: Vatican I
              Vatican II
              Personal Spiritual History of Candidate
  4. Liturgy
      A. Community Approach
      B. Personal Involvement
  5. Scripture
      A. History
      B. Prayer
  6. Practice

Session III

The Sacraments: The Christian Person Grows:
Seven View Points
Intro: Status as Candidate!
      What is a Christian?

  1. Liturgical
    Ritual of Sacraments
  2. Scriptural
    God and Man in Consort
  3. Community Significance
    Togetherness
    Status
    Individuality
  4. Pragmatics
    Encounter
    Involvement
Personal Satisfaction
  5. Historically: Church
              Civilization
              Personal

Session IV (With Parents)
    Introduction: Together at Baptism
                     Together at Mass
    1. Baptism
        A. Liturgy
            New Unique Person
            Creation of Love: God and Man
            Potential
            Guarantees
            Ritual
        B. Scripture: Directive of Christ
        C. History
        D. Community
        E. Personalism of Church
    2. Holy Eucharist
        A. Modern Method at Mass
        B. Difficulties and Objections
        C. History
        D. Decree on "The Liturgy"
        E. Practicalities
        F. Assignments

Session V
    Intro: Confession in the Now Church As An Adult
    1. New Approach:
        A. Negative
            Encounter with Priest—Christ—Community
            Psychological Aspect
            Emotional Realities
            Understanding: Nature of Sin
        B. Positive
            Same Encounter but Greater Realism
            As an Adult—Christian Child's Approach is
            OUT

2. History
   A. Early Church
   B. 4th to 11th Century
3. Necessity for Instruction
   Difficulties
   Penance as Virtue
4. Universal Duty of Christian in Vocation to Unity
   with Christ
   Honest Humility
   Hope and Mercy
   Revolve with Love
5. Modern Techniques
   Development of and Education of the Christian
   Conscience
   The Positive Approach: Encounter with God and
   Community
   Levels: Instinctual—Conscious—Decisive—Con-
   viction
6. Post Vatican II
   Theme: Encounter: God
                      Person
                      Community
   One of Many Encounters
   As Member of Mission — Pilgrim Church
   Personal Work of the Church
   Participation in Mystery of Christ Redeeming
   the World
Introduction: Confirmation
   Adulthood: Spiritually
              Emotionally
   A. Liturgy
      Community Reception
      Ritual
      Minister

B. History
    Social Aspects
    Family Vision
    Modern Requirements
C. Scripture
    Holy Spirit
    Effects of Sacrament
D. Pragmatics
    Name
    Sponsor
    Preparation

Session VI
    Marriage and Priesthood
    Introduction: As Adults We Live and Pray Socially
A. Qualifications
    Spiritual
    Emotional
B. Marriage
    1. Setting: God's Community
    2. Ritual: The Wedding
    3. Encounter: Person and Christ
    4. Statistics
    5. Vows — Rings — Blessings
C. Priesthood
    1. Nomination — By People
    2. Charge: People
            Candidate
    3. Ritual: Imposition
            Anointing
    4. Lay Priesthood: Now Church
    5. Preparation

Second Semester

Session I

　　General Schema
　　Adult Christian Person (see Outline I)
　　A.　Role of Adult
　　　　1.　Scripture
　　　　2.　History
　　B.　Living the Role
　　　　1.　Service: Church/Community
　　　　2.　Prayer Life
　　C.　Attitudes: Maturity
　　D.　Difficulties
　　E.　Role in New Church
　　　　Decrees: Church in Modern World
　　　　　　Laity
　　　　　　Ecumenism
　　　　　　Mission, etc.
　　F.　Role of Parents — Sponsors
　　G.　Practice

Session II

　　Dignity and Respect
　　A.　Good Manners: Sign of Confidence and Comfort
　　B.　Awareness of Status
　　C.　Spiritual Basis
　　　　Law of Love: God and Neighbor
　　D.　Pratical Awareness
　　E.　Refinement of Legalism
　　F.　New Dimensions:　Sensitivity
　　　　　　　　　　　　　　Security
　　G.　Qualities:　Refinement
　　　　　　　　　　　Delicacy
　　H.　Integrity
　　 I.　Honest Humility

Session III
Sexuality
Introduction: Mature, Dignified Adult Christian
A. Sex and Sexuality
B. Adult Involvement
C. Dynamics
D. Totality
E. Complementarity
F. Faith and Understanding
G. Demands: Trust — Respect
H. Aspects: Emotional — Spiritual
I. Problems
J. Cautions

Session IV (With Parents)
Introduction: Mature Christian Person Has Joy
A. Joy at Freedom from Childishness
B. Freedom for:
    1. Love: Self and Another
    2. Development — Developing
    3. Vocation: Marriage
                 Religion
    4. Holy Spirit: Wisdom
                      Strength
    5. New Directions
    6. Confirmation

Session V
Obedience
Introduction: Mature Christian Adult Expects and
    Gives
Obedience
A. Freedom Gives and Demands
    From: Home — School — Church

123

To: Home — School — Church
B. Virtue of Obedience
C. Price of Obedience
   Unity
   Freedom
   Privacy
   Love
D. Practice
E. Study

Session VI
   Authority
   Introduction: Freedom and Obedience Demand
                  Authority
A. Basic Requirements:
   Responsibility of Adulthood
   Jurisdiction
   Collegiality
   Subsidiarity
B. Use and Abuse
C. Practical Items:
   Cars
   Money
   Drugs — Alcohol
   Clothes
   Sex
D. Insurance: Dialogue
   Maturity
   Study
   Meditation

6/ MARRIAGE

The Reverend Joseph M. Champlin has done a masterful job in giving us the text *Together for Life,* published by Ave Maria Press, Notre Dame, Indiana. His expert liturgical arrangement of this Sacrament, coupled with his sophisticated commentary, is all we need to help our young people to get off to a good start in marriage.

The liturgy of the wedding, actually constructed by the bride and groom, is a demonstration of the principle of personalism in the now Church. The dialogue that they, the bride and groom, have had together with their priest in the preparation of their wedding has made them secure in their understanding of the Church's concern for them. The occasion of the wedding is more than a celebration of love by the bride and groom with their family and friends. Over and above being a "teachable moment" for the whole community, a wedding in a family is a most critical time for the parents of the bride and groom. These people have been the subject of innumerable stories, plays, and television series and TV commercials. Seldom, if ever, have they been more than the object of ridicule in juvenile situation comedy. The wedding of a son or daughter in God's family demands that the Church gives the parents of the bride and groom some special treatment. As a concluding notation in this manual I would like to outline the specifics of this special treatment that I have found helpful to them at this important time in their lives. The emphasis of this little program is on the role of the parents of the bride and groom. After the conference has been held, the subject matter could well serve as a delicate and sensitive source of discussion for all six people.

The idea of a conference for parents was well defined some years ago by a member of the "Cana Conference." I would like to see the idea resurrected now and used to further demonstrate the personalism of the now Church.

The principle of "personalism" is possibly more important to parents at the time of the marriage of their child than it was at the Baptism; for them, as well as for the bride and groom. All one has to do is to look, during the wedding, over the heads of the bride and groom into the faces of their parents to see the need of these people for special treatment. They are very concerned, even worried about the new family of God that is being created. They know full well that their love and God created the person ready to commit himself/herself to someone for life. They want, they hope that this new family will be a success in God's and our community. They expect to help as much as they can to effect this end. They have faith in God and in their child. They tried as hard as they could to prepare their child for this great step. Now they themselves are lonesome. All the champagne in the world will not make them as comfortable as they should be, but a few moments with God's minister will bring them the strength and comfort they need.

All four of the parents, given the usual situation, are facing a moment of truth. Having seen their person come of age, legally and morally, and attach himself/herself to another is expected. At the same time it is almost shocking. It could cause an ulcer and often does. These people know the meaning of privacy. They want very much to allow their child and his/her love to enjoy it. They have every intention of minding their own business. They understand the meaning of these words from *Together for Life* . . . "The parents' task is over. Now they can only sit back, watch, and hope that their years of loving concern have produced a mature young man or woman. . . ." No matter how well imbued they are with this mentality, the rigors and pitfalls to which their children will be subjected to in modern marriage, will necessitate discussion and constant awareness of the real role that they the parents must play in time of stress or strife. This must be the primary subject of their discussion with each other and their priest.

A conference of this nature has an unusually optimistic tone. It carries with it the presumption that the candidates for marriage are in fact quite capable of adjusting to the demands of married life. The parents are well aware of the personal attention their children have received from the Church in preparation for their marriage. Not one of them is about to say that the bride or groom is a selfish, stubborn juvenile. Besides they must be realists. They must examine and discuss the incident of failure in modern marriage by reason of parental interference or total lack of concern in their children's married life. These are very sensitive issues and must be discussed with a great deal of tact, but the discussion will bear fruit. Honesty and integrity demonstrated before the wedding can allay a great deal of harm later.

This conference with the parents of the bride and groom is, in fact, a demonstration of the Church's concern for everybody. It is the Church's personalism in practice. As such it expects a response from the people. The response we expect is, as it was with the other Sacraments, a total family commitment.

It could well be the case that neither of the parents of either bride or groom ever made a commitment to God or to the Church. As we mentioned earlier in our chapter on Baptism, they really saw no need of it, or worse, did not even think of it. This is another chance we have to demonstrate "personalism." They know how concerned we are about their children. They have seen the special treatment the bride and groom are receiving. They may have even looked at or read *Together for Life*. If they are talked with now — at this teachable moment — they may just have decided to start going to church, and to become committed Christians. If they are already with us completely, they will simply enjoy the short conference all the more. These people deserve it and can profit most by it.

Our conference at this time in the life of the parents is not unlike the baptismal conference that we spoke of in the beginning of this manual. The liturgy provides the vehicle for collegial dialogue in God's family.

At the conference, when you read to them the final blessing given at Baptism to the mother and father, and recall to them the covenant they made with God to take good care of their child, physically and spiritually, they will well remember it. The wedding day then will be a time to renew this covenant. When you bring to their minds the fact that they have nourished their child with the bread of life in the Holy Eucharist, their own eucharistic mentality takes on a deeper meaning. How with the adulthood of their children at hand, they must be aware of the lonesomeness that will be theirs in the immediate future. This lonesomeness is not unlike that of the Holy Couple, Mary and Joseph, when Christ Himself left them to be about His Father's business. The parallelism, I think, is not too farfetched. In any case, they can appreciate what we are talking about and make their lonesomeness a daily prayer. The answer to their prayer, of course, will be the birth of a grandchild at which time the cycle starts again. Hopefully, they will have transmitted the theme that we are a Church family, that we are totally committed to God and His Church, and completely relaxed and happy in it.

7/ CONCLUSION

In reviewing all the programs of this manual, I find specific benefits for the minister and for his people. In conclusion, I would like to make a few final, brief remarks.

In an effort to demonstrate the conciliar theme of personalism to God's people at these important times in their lives, the priest redefines and emphasizes his own identity in his liturgical ministry. Some of this truly sacerdotal identity has been overshadowed and even belittled, no doubt unwittingly, by an exaggerated sense of the importance of other ministries in the Church. In the past few years the ordinary parish priest with his sacramental ministry has been given a back seat by "experts" in the Church — would-be theologians, psychologists and sociologists. The personalism of these programs for himself and his people gives the priest a status that is most important to himself and to the Church. Herein is his real identity as a priest with his people.

A priest who has this comfortable, relaxed attitude toward his office will do a great deal for the Church and his people. We must understand just how important these times are for the people. By his attitude he can literally dissolve many of the criticisms of the people who do not understand, as well as they might, the now Church and all that this implies. By his personal involvement with his people he can demonstrate to the whole Church a new spirit of loyalty and dedication to the basics of the living, praying Church. This quiet involvement with his people will not put his name in *Who's Who*, nor his picture on the cover of a news magazine, but it will create in the Church the quiet, growing spirit that we need so much in our modern Church. It may even be a real factor in dissipating a spirit of competition in clerical ranks that is so destructive to our priestly office.

I wrote this manual for a basically selfish motive. I wanted to correlate many different approaches to the solution of the problems of our modern Church. I was fatigued with the enumerable, often untried, suggestions offered by many theorists in the Church. This compilation of programs, I think, will save a great deal of our time, talent and tithe.

Over the years I have also become tired of being used or exploited by some of the people in the community. I was most reluctant to "wipe the dust" from a "stiff-necked generation" until I had provided every opportunity I could give them. I think the programs in this manual do just that.

Our people have been confused at times in our now Church. They need shepherds who care for each one of them. We can, with a bit of love and efficiency, show them just how much we do care for them. We are the Church, and so are they. The bond of love between us can only grow stronger as we live together at these teachable moments.

Part II
Ritual of Prayers and Blessings

INTRODUCTION

This ritual, in conjunction with *Sacraments in the New Liturgy,* is presented to priests and other ministers of the Gospel in this country as a handy text for use in everyday parish living. It contains many prayers and blessings that can be used at critical moments of importance to us, our people, and the Church.

It is presented as a means, an effort, to update and regain some of the piety that was so evident in the preconciliar Church. This piety has not been lost. It has been perhaps hidden in our churches in recent years. It must now be given the occasion to emerge.

Many of the prayers and blessings will be familiar to all. Some have been changed in wording and meaning. Some have been shortened or lengthened depending on the particular situation. There have been many fonts from which to draw. Some are original. It is of no matter. It will provide us with the essential means to demonstrate to our people the present situation — liturgically speaking — that we have not discarded any of the ancient and honorable, nor have we hesitated to look to the new and applicable.

There are a great many prayers in the new *Sacramentary* but one wonders how often they will be referred to, practically speaking, outside the actual celebration of the Eucharistic liturgy. This ritual will be a ready text to use in the community for times and occasions which are of special concern to our people. The litanies and prayers included at the end of the ritual provide us with an abbreviated form for more use in our churches on special occasions.

The order in which the prayers and blessings have been arranged corresponds to Part I of the book. Death, being the birth into the everlasting, comes first.

The rest of the prayers and blessings follow in a somewhat natural order. Many of the prayers must be said with or in a group as the collegial family of God at prayer. Others, of course, can be offered by the individual. In any event, they can certainly provide a sharp point of meditation for all.

8/ LITURGY FOR SPECIAL OCCASIONS

DAY OF DEATH

PSALM 102
O Lord, hear my prayer, and let my cry come to You.
Hide not Your face from me in this day of my distress
For my days vanish like smoke and my bones burn like
fire, withered and dried up
Like grass is my heart, because of my sighing I am re-
duced to skin and bone
I am sleepless, I am like a sparrow alone on the house-
top.

PRAYER
O my Father, today is the worst day of my life. I am confused. I am shocked. I am angry. I am sick. Why did this
happen to me? Why did You not warn me? Why should I
be the one to lose my dear love? My dear God, today I
give you my lonesomeness. Now I will be alone. I give

You my tiredness. Now I will not have the help I need. I give You my guilt. I should have loved him/her more. I give You my selfishness. Now I can't have the one I want. But I believe and I know that You will send someone to me to help me in this time of trouble. Amen.

SCRIPTURE
Do not let your heart be troubled. Have faith in God and faith in me. In my Father's house there are many rooms. Otherwise how could I have told you that I was going to prepare a room for you. I am indeed going to prepare a room for you and then I shall come back to take you with me, that where I am you also may be.

DAY AFTER THE FUNERAL

PSALM 130
Out of the depths I cry to you, O Lord. Lord, hear my voice. If you, O Lord, mark iniquities, Lord, who can stand. But with You is forgiveness that You may be revered. I trust in the Lord. My soul trusts in His Word. My soul waits for the Lord. For with the Lord is kindness and with Him is redemption.

PRAYER
My dear Father, today is not as bad as the other day was but I am still confused. I feel numb. I feel weak. But Your peace and grace are with me. My dear God, today I give You my emptiness, my dryness, my aching body and spirit. With your help, I will pray, with my beloved, every day, until we are together again, In You, in Heaven. Amen.

SCRIPTURE

When the Son of Man comes in His glory, escorted by all the angels of Heaven, He will sit upon His royal throne, and all the nations will be assembled before Him. He will separate them into two groups, as a shepherd separates sheep from goats. The sheep He will place on His right hand, the goats on His left. The King will say to those on His right, "Come, you have my Father's blessings. Inherit the kingdom prepared for you from the creation of the world. For I was hungry and You gave me food, I was thirsty and You gave me drink. I was a stranger and You welcomed me, naked and You clothed me. I was sick and You comforted me, in prison, and you came to visit me. Then the good people will ask Him: Lord when did we see You hungry and feed You? Or see You thirsty and give You drink? When did we welcome You away from home? Or clothe You in Your nakedness? When did we visit You when You were ill or in prison? The King will answer them, I tell you, solemnly, as often as you did it for one of my least brothers or sisters, you did it for me.

A BLESSING OF CHILDREN
AT TIME OF A DEATH IN THE FAMILY

O Almighty God, pour down Thy tender blessings on these, our children, now, when they need them so much. May their tears be an offering to You. May their pain be taken away by our love for them, and may they be able, some day, to understand this mystery of death. Amen.

PRAYER WITH A CHILD AT TIME OF A DEATH

Dear God, please take care of my good and holy father (mother — brother — sister). When I come to Heaven I will help you to take care of him/her. I don't know why you took him/her to Heaven, now. I love You, God. I will

be good. I love daddy/mommy, too. I will be lonesome.
So I will pray with him/her every day. Amen.

WHEN A CHILD DIES IN UTERO (IN BIRTH)
PRAYER WITH MOTHER AND FATHER OF CHILD
Oh God, our hands and arms are empty.
Our hearts and souls are empty.
We wanted so much to touch our baby before You took
him/her to Heaven. We were going to call him/her N.
Now we will call him/her Saint N. We do not know what
to do now. Mary and Joseph, please help us. Amen.

9/   PRAYERS AND BLESSINGS

INTRODUCTORY PRAYER

Almighty and everlasting God, who conferred on Your
priests, above all others, so great a grace, that whatever
they do in Your name, is regarded as being done by You,
We pray that in Your kindness You may be present wherever we are present. May You bless whatever we bless.
At our lowly coming, may the merits and prayers of Your
saints be with us, and May the angel of peace be at your
hand, through Christ our Lord, Amen.

PRAYER FOR FORMAL OCCASIONS

O Almighty God, You have dominion over the living and
the dead. You are merciful to all who acknowledge You
by faith and by good work. We humbly ask You to pour
forth Your blessings upon us and to look with favor upon

the thoughts, desires and plans which have arisen in our hearts. In Your goodness, grant us joyful remembrance of this occasion. We make our prayer through Christ our Lord, Amen.

BLESSING OF A HOUSE

May the peace of Christ come with us into this house. May it extend to all who pass through these doors.

O Almighty God, strengthen the foundation of this house. Its family is built on the rock of faith. May it stand secure through weather foul and fair.

Brighten the name on the mailbox of the man and woman who are the head and the heart of this family. Give them the true and real spirit of hospitality to be gracious to all their guests in this living room.

You will be their favorite guest at every meal they serve at this table.

May their checkbook always have sufficient funds registered — and balance.

May the well never run dry —

May the cupboard never be bare —

May the facilities always function —

May the beds bring rest and repose to tired minds and bodies —

And may the mortgage soon be burned.

O Holy Spirit, help the children of this family to learn love and happiness in this house. It is your very special little school and church.

PRAYER FOR A WEDDING ANNIVERSARY

O almighty God, look with kindness on these children of Yours, Who in gladness
Give thanks to You today for the joys of their life together.

They are happy that they have put all their hopes in You and in each other.
Bless them, Lord, their loved ones, and their dear friends Who are here,
So that they may know they are blessed in Your eyes and in the eyes of Your people.

O God, whose mercy is unlimited, and whose goodness is inexhaustible, we thank You for all that You have given us, especially at this time. For the example of a blessed couple who have walked in the law of the Lord. All that they have asked for, in Your design, You have given them.
And we know that You have prepared them for an eternal reward. Continue to look with favor upon them and the rest of us.
May this occasion continue to be joyous through our resolve to be diligent in Your service as our dear friends have been.
We make our prayer through Christ our Lord, Amen.

BLESSING OF PARENTS OF A BRIDE AND GROOM

Pour down Thy blessings, O Almighty God, on this good man and woman. You have sanctified their love for many years now. You helped them to live as Your children, sharing their common life under Your fatherly care. Now, give them the grace to give their child in marriage, with the security of the self-sacrifice with which they started their own marriage.
And may they see their children's children to the third and fourth generation. Amen.

BLESSING OF A RING

O Almighty God, bless the gold of this ring that is as pure as the faith that gave it (and the sparkling jewel that shines as the love that received it). Bless the finger that will be encircled by this ring. It will be the constant reminder of all that it symbolizes, the sign of the thoughts of the one who gave it and the one who wears it. Its brightness and warmth will show to all who see it, the presence of Your love among us. May it be the sweet reminder of sacred memories, happy or sad, to help us appreciate all Your blessings. We ask this through Christ our Lord. Amen.

BLESSING OF A PREGNANCY

O Almighty God, help us to understand the mystery of the conception of this beloved child. We know this child, be it boy or girl, has been the result of the love You gave this holy man and woman for You and for each other. As Mary and Joseph awaited the birth of Jesus with joy, fatigue and concern, so also will this happy couple. We ask You to give them the patience that they need and the relaxed quiet that will help them. May they both, the heart and head of this family, grow every day more in love with each other, as they wait for the joyous day You have made for the birth of their child. Amen.

PRAYER WITH COUPLE

Our Father Who art in Heaven and in our home, by Your love and by our power, with our bodies and with Your grace, this baby is ours. We ask You to help us to get ready for the day that You have made for the birth of our baby. We ask this through our Lord and His Mother. Amen.

BLESSING

I bless with God's grace this home of yours.
I bless the cellar and the roof.
I bless the bed and the cradle that will hold your baby.
And I bless everybody who lives here. Amen.
Our souls proclaim the greatness of the Lord; our spirits rejoice in God our Savior; because He has looked on the humility of His son and daughter. The Almighty has done great things for us; Holy is His name, and blessed are His people.

BEFORE FIRST COMMUNION
PRAYER WITH CHILD

Dear Jesus: I am ready to make my first Holy Communion.
I am not worried. I know what I am doing.
I love my mother.
I love my father.
I love my priest-father.
And now, I can love You and them more. Amen.

BLESSING

May God bless the parents of this child, the first and the best of teachers in the ways of faith.
May our Lord come to this child and fill his/her heart with love:

And may the Holy Spirit guide us all, as our family grows closer together, in our love of God. Amen.

PRAYER FOR YOUNG PEOPLE

O most holy Creator, we thank You for Your help while the thoughts of our young people — and desires for their holy growth have been first in our minds and hearts. Do not let any misunderstanding mar the harmony of spirit with which we love each other. Do grant us, however, a holy rivalry in our efforts to lead our young people to lives which will mirror the image of God for all to see. Grant, O Lord, through the intercession of Mary Immaculate, that our young people be preserved from the world's harm. We ask this through Christ our Lord. Amen.

PRAYER FOR GRADUATION EXERCISES

O Lord God, You have called us to the vocation of being a source of edification to those whom You have brought into the world after us. We humble ourselves in Your presence, as we heartily recommend to You our dear graduates. We entrust them to Your all powerful protection.

We pray that they may grow daily in Your love.
To the best of our ability we have tried to instill in their hearts the Christian way of life. They know that all their efforts will be to no avail unless You, almighty and merciful God, make them fruitful by Your heavenly blessing. Bless them, Master, we pray. Amen.

BLESSING OF THE PARENTS
OF A SICK CHILD

O Almighty God, please put some strength into the heads and hearts of the parents of this sick child. They are as sick as Your child is. We pray that our will be Yours on earth as it is in Heaven; that this child of ours gets better. We pray in the name of Mary and Joseph and Your Son, Jesus. Amen.

PRAYER FOR A SICK INFANT
WITH PARENTS

O Almighty God, take from our baby this sickness that is gripping him (her). He is so small, he is helpless. We, ourselves, are sick with fear and worry in our hearts. We have faith in You and love for our baby. We know You will give us the strength we need, until we have our baby back home with us in good health. We ask St. Elizabeth and St. Zachary to pray for us. They knew Jesus, Your Son, as a child and they see our family in this mystery of pain. "Come and make our child better." Amen.

PRAYER BEFORE SURGERY

O Almighty God, with faith and confidence, we put our trust in Your divine will. Without regard for the worry we have, or the seriousness of this coming operation, we know we are now and forever in Your hands. We pray for our doctors and nurses: give to their hands Your holy skill; give to their heads and hearts Your concern for their patient. With Your grace and their care, Your patient will be restored to good health, and once more be able to join our family at home, at work, and in church. We pray to Your doctor, St. Luke. We ask him to help the rest of the family at home in their lonesomeness and fatigue. All of us offer You our pain, our fears, and our love. Please help us, through Christ, our Lord. Amen.

PRAYER WITH A PERSON
AFTER SURGERY

O Almighty God, we give You our relaxed thanks for Your blessings and help. We are most grateful now that this ordeal is over. We praise You, in Your providence, for bringing us to this point of progress. We offer You our pain. We offer You our impatience. We offer you the bother our convalescence will demand. We thank You for the skill of our doctors and nurses. Bless them always. Continue to give added strength to our body every day, so that our trust in You can also grow and increase with our good health. We pray through Christ our Lord. Amen.

PRAYER FOR THE ALTAR SOCIETY

Grant, O Lord, that, as we prepare to put our plans into action, we be mindful that God's house is a place that purifies, elevates and inspires our souls. It must be kept as a fitting place for the majestic liturgy of the Church, our public worship, which is the fount of the true Christian spirit. May we be granted the strength so to do our work that our Church will have nothing pretentious or false about it. May it have simplicity and sincerity as its chief characteristic. Grant us simplicity in ourselves in what we do and may God be with us on our way. Amen.

PRAYER FOR A CHURCH SOCIETY

O Lord, grant that the offerings that we make now, of all our words and actions on this occasion, be acceptable to You. May this holy interchange of love between You and us unite forever our human nature with Your divine Will. Our final petition to You is that we be granted the favor of realizing that our society, established by Your Church, is to be loved as a source of divine grace. Amen.

BLESSING OF A LECTOR

O Lord grant that this person may see and understand Your holy words. Give him/her the power of speech to proclaim the thoughts of the prophets and the strength of voice to announce the message of the Apostles. Make him/her feel the role of leadership he/she has in Your family gathered together to praise Your name and ask for Your blessings. Together with his/her priest and filled with humble and relaxed competency he/she will gather into one voice of song and word all the offerings of Your people. May they be the best of offerings from Your family to You, our most loving Father. Amen.

BLESSING OF THE CHOIR

O Almighty God, grant that we may all sing to the Lord a new canticle of love. So that His praise may resound in the assembly of the saints. May the liturgy purify our hearts so that we may ever desire to sing festively in Your presence. May the world be ordered with peace so that all may some day serve You in joyful devotion. We ask this through Christ, our Lord. Amen.

BLESSING OF ALTAR BOYS

With all our hearts and voices, we bless You, God the Father, the Son and the Holy Spirit. Grant, O merciful Trinity, to our altar boys an ardent desire to keep themselves attached to You and to Your altar of sacrifice. May neither the difficulties of life nor the joys of youth change their determination to be friends of Christ, and protectors of His holy table. May their hearts ever be generous and upright and their minds alert, always ready for You. Amen.

BLESSING FOR USHERS

O God, Who has prepared for us, who love You, such good things as eye has not seen, pour into our hearts Your divine love so that we may have the grace to appreciate having an official part in the worship of our Church. St. Paul called himself in Scripture a "Servant of God." St. Jude glorifies in the title "Servant of Jesus Christ." Bless our efforts every time we are here in this church so that we may imitate the holy ones of Christ. Amen.

BLESSING OF FIELDS AND PASTURES

O Almighty God, from Whom every good thing has its beginning,
And from Whom it receives its increase
Send forth Your spirit and all things shall be created.
We beg You to hear our prayers,
We beg that You bless these fields,
We beg that you protect these pastures.
Consecrate these meadows and mountains

150

and protect them from all destruction.
In Your mercy, ward off and dispel all lightning, hail and harmful floods.
And we ask this through Christ our Lord. Amen.

BLESSING OF AN ORCHARD OR VINEYARD

O Almighty God we appeal to Your kindness,
Asking that You pour out the dew of Your blessings
On These budding creatures of Yours
Which it has pleased You to nurture with rain and mild breezes.
We ask that You bring the fruit of Your earth to a ripe harvest.
For Your people we ask a spirit of constant gratitude for Your gifts.
From a fertile earth, fill the hungry with an abundance of good things, so that the poor and the needy may praise Your wondrous deeds, forever and ever. Amen.

BLESSING OF A BRIDGE

O Lord, listen to our prayers and be pleased to bless this bridge and all who pass over it.
May they ever find in You a safeguard among the joys and sorrows of this fickle world.
Hear us, Holy Lord and Father, Almighty God,
And in Your goodness send Your holy angel from Heaven to watch over,
to protect and support this bridge and bless all who pass over and under it.
We ask this through Christ our Lord. Amen.

BLESSING OF A FACTORY

O Lord God Almighty, by the coming of Your only begotten Son to this earth, You sanctified all things for Your faithful people. We beg You to bless this factory and to protect Your people who work here from every kind of adversity and accident, temptation and trial. Grant that they may do their work well so that it is a means of their salvation, and a help for their families. May they be living and chosen stones in the everlasting dwelling of Your majesty. We ask this through Christ our Lord. Amen.

BLESSING OF A CAR (TRUCK OR AIRCRAFT)

O Lord we ask You to bless this car (truck, aircraft). We trust You have guided the people who made it, so that it will be safe and secure in performance. More especially we ask You to bless its drivers (pilots).
We ask you to give them energy and accuracy, so that they may drive (fly) with efficiency for themselves and their passengers.
Give them safety from the moment they leave until the time they return.
Give them security in all kinds of weather.
Give them joy, satisfaction and rest on their return.
We ask this through Christ, our Lord. Amen.

BLESSING OF A SHIP OR A FLEET

O Lord, listen to our prayers and by Your holy hand
Bless this ship (this fleet)
Its passengers, this captain and this crew.
As You were pleased to bless Peter's bark

Reach out Your hand, O Lord, now.
Send Your holy angel from on high to watch over it and all on board.
Ward off any threat of disaster and guide its course through calm waters to safe harbors.
Then, when they have successfully transacted their business,
May You and Your loving providence bring them back with glad hearts
To their own country and home port.
We ask this of You who live and reign forever and ever. Amen.

BLESSING OF A MOTORCYCLE

O Almighty God, we ask You to bless this bike.
With complete trust in the skill You have given to its manufacturers, we now beg for safety for its rider(s).
Give clear, straightforward vision to its operator.
Give to all who ride it, a quality of control that will keep everybody safe and secure.
Give them the good sense to follow all regulations and thus enjoy and use this unique and efficient way of travel.
We ask this blessing through Christ, our Lord. Amen.

PRAYER FOR A POLITICAL OCCASION

With constant dependence on our Creator,
For the spiritual gifts required in the conduct of our affairs,
As individuals and a nation,
We ask Almighty God for the wisdom and strength to ful-

fill the high purposes for which we are called.
Seeking the welfare of all people,
Through a just and lasting peace upon the face of this earth,
And desiring happiness for the humblest family and for the homes of the mighty, We pray
With eager expectation,
That all people may be inspired to sacrifice at home and abroad
To achieve a life worthy of the children of God, now and forever. Amen.

BLESSING AND/OR DEDICATION
OF A LABOR UNION

O Almighty God, all of us gathered here once more consecrate to You our hearts and our hands. We call upon St. Joseph, the patron of workers, to fill us with the spirit of solidarity that we profess by this meeting. We have paid our dues by the time and worry we have for ourselves, our families, and for our industry. You know the dangers of decision that are with us. You know the concern of our families at home. Take from us all hostility so that in agreement with all parties involved, we may share with all, the justice and the profits of our labors. Let us enjoy all Your blessings while we work together. Amen.

MEMORIAL SERVICE
FOR MILITARY PERSONNEL

O Lord God, King of Martyrs, comfort to the afflicted,
Support and consolation to all those who suffer,
In Your kindness, hear our fervent prayers for our honored dead.

Bless these exercises held by a grateful people.
Grant that by looking backward on our heritage of valor,
We may be strengthened, in our determination,
To hand down to the next generation a burning patriotism,
So that their hearts may be on fire with a love of God,
A love of country, and a love of their fellow men.
These men and women offered their lives on the altar of their country and it is fitting that every American revere them.
May the heart of America ever throb deep, firm and true for those who died that we may live. Amen.

LITANY OF THE SACRED HEART OF JESUS

Lord, have mercy on us.

Christ, have mercy on us.

Holy Trinity, one God, have mercy on us.

Heart of Jesus, formed by the Holy Spirit in the womb of the Virgin Mother, have mercy on us.

Heart of Jesus, Burning Furnace of charity, have mercy on us.

Heart of Jesus, King and Center of all hearts, have mercy on us.

Heart of Jesus, in whom are all the treasures of wisdom and knowledge, have mercy on us.

Heart of Jesus, patient and most merciful, have mercy on us.

Heart of Jesus, pierced with a lance, have mercy on us.

Heart of Jesus, Source of all consolation, have mercy on us.

Heart of Jesus, Salvation of all those who trust in You, have mercy on us.

Heart of Jesus, Hope of those who die in You, have mercy on us.

Heart of Jesus, Delight of all the saints, have mercy on us.

Lamb of God, Who takes away the sins of the world, spare us, O Lord.

Lamb of God, Who takes away the sins of the world, graciously hear us, O Lord.

Lamb of God, Who takes away the sins of the world, have mercy on us.

Jesus meek and humble of heart, make our hearts like unto Thine.

Let us pray. O Almighty and eternal God, look upon the heart of Your dearly beloved Son and, upon the praise and satisfaction He offers You on behalf of sinners. Grant pardon to those who seek Your mercy, in the name of the same Jesus Christ. Amen.

LITANY OF OUR BLESSED VIRGIN MARY

Lord, have mercy on us.

Christ, have mercy on us.

Holy Trinity, one God, have mercy on us.

Holy Mary, pray for us.

Holy Mother of God, pray for us.

Holy Virgin of virgins, pray for us.

Mother, most pure, pray for us.

Mother of good counsel, pray for us.

Virgin most prudent, pray for us.

Virgin most faithful, pray for us.

Mirror of justice, pray for us.

Seat of wisdom, pray for us.

Tower of ivory, pray for us.

House of God, pray for us.

Gate of Heaven, pray for us.
Morning star, pray for us.
Queen of angels, pray for us.
Queen, conceived without original sin, pray for us.
Queen of peace, pray for us.
Lamb of God who takes away the sins of the world, spare us, O Lord.
Lamb of God who takes away the sins of the world, graciously hear us, O Lord.
Lamb of God who takes away the sins of the world, have mercy on us.
Pray for us, O holy Mother of God, that we may be made worthy of the promises of Christ.
Let us pray. Grant us, Your servants, we beseech You, O Lord, continual health of body and soul; and through the glorious intercession of the Blessed Mary, ever virgin, may we be delivered from present sorrows, and given eternal happiness. We ask this through Christ our Lord. Amen.

LITANY OF ST. JOSEPH

Lord, have mercy on us.
Christ, have mercy on us.
Holy Trinity, one God, have mercy on us.
Holy Mary, pray for us.
St. Joseph, pray for us.
Spouse of the Mother of God, pray for us.
Guardian of the Virgin, pray for us.
Foster Father of the Son of God, pray for us.
Joseph, most obedient, pray for us.
Model of workers, pray for us.
Pillar of families, pray for us.
Patron of the dying, pray for us.

Protector of Holy Church, pray for us.

Lamb of God, who takes away the sins of the world, spare us O Lord.

Lamb of God, who takes away the sins of the world, graciously hear us O Lord.

Lamb of God, who takes away the sins of the world, have mercy on us.

God made Him the Lord of His household and the Prince over all His possessions.

Let us pray. O God, You selected blessed Joseph to be the husband of Your Most Holy Mother.

Grant, we ask, to be worthy to have him for our patron in Heaven, whom on earth we venerate as our protector. We ask this through Christ our Lord and His Mother. Amen.

LITANY OF THE SAINTS

Lord, have mercy.

Christ, have mercy.

Holy Trinity, one God, have mercy on us.

Holy Mary, pray for us.

St. Michael, pray for us.

St. John the Baptist, pray for us.

St. Joseph, pray for us.

St. Peter, pray for us.

St. Paul, pray for us.

St. Stephen, pray for us.

St. Lawrence, pray for us.

St. Gregory, pray for us.

St. Augustine, pray for us.

St. Jerome, pray for us.

St. Bernard, pray for us.

St. Dominic, pray for us.

St. Francis, pray for us.

St. Mary Magdalen, pray for us.

St. Agnes, pray for us.

St. Catherine, pray for us.

From all evil, deliver us, O Lord. From all sin, deliver us, O Lord. By the mystery of Your holy incarnation, deliver us, O Lord. By Your birth, deliver us, O Lord. By Your cross and passion, deliver us, O Lord. By Your holy resurrection, deliver us, O Lord. By the coming of the Holy Spirit, deliver us, O Lord.

Lamb of God, You take away the sins of the world, spare us, O Lord.

Lamb of God, You take away the sins of the world, graciously hear us, O Lord.

Lamb of God, You take away the sins of the world, have mercy on us.

Let us pray. O God, from whom come all holy desires, right counsels and good works, give to Your servants that peace which the world cannot give. May our hearts be dedicated to the observance of Your law as were the hearts of all Your saints. When we are freed from the fear of our enemies and tranquil in the knowledge of Your protection, may we join them in Heaven with You to live forever, in Your love. Amen.